6. Enter your class ID code to join a class.

YOU HAVE A CLASS ID CODE FROM YOUR TEACHER

a. Enter your class code and click [Next]

b. Students in a class can use the Discussion Board and Email tools.

c. To enter the class ID code later, choose **Join a Class**.

YOU DO NOT HAVE A CLASS ID CODE

a. You do not need a class ID code to use *iQ Online*. Click [Skip]

b. To enter the class ID code later, choose **Join a Class**.

7. Check your registration information and click Log In. Then choose your book. Click **Activities** to begin using *iQ Online*.

IMPORTANT

- After you register, the next time you want to use *iQ Online*, go to www.iQOnlinePractice.com. Log in with your email address and password.

- You can use *iQ Online* for 12 months from the date you register.

- For help, please contact customer service: eltsupport@oup.com.

OXFORD
UNIVERSITY PRESS

198 Madison Avenue
New York, NY 10016 USA

Great Clarendon Street, Oxford, OX2 6DP, United Kingdom

Oxford University Press is a department of the University of Oxford.
It furthers the University's objective of excellence in research, scholarship,
and education by publishing worldwide. Oxford is a registered trade
mark of Oxford University Press in the UK and in certain other countries

First published in 2015
2019 2018 2017
10 9 8 7 6 5 4 3

No unauthorized photocopying

Adult Content Director: Stephanie Karras
Publisher: Sharon Sargent
Managing Editor: Mariel DeKranis
Development Editor: Eric Zuarino
Executive Art and Design Manager: Maj-Britt Hagsted
Design Project Manager: Debbie Lofaso
Content Production Manager: Julie Armstrong
Image Manager: Trisha Masterson
Image Editor: Liaht Ziskind
Production Coordinator: Brad Tucker

ISBN: 978 0 19 481805 6 Student Book intro with iQ Online pack
ISBN: 978 0 19 481806 3 Student Book intro as pack component
ISBN: 978 0 19 481802 5 iQ Online student website

Printed in China
This book is printed on paper from certified and well-managed sources.

ACKNOWLEDGEMENTS

Illustrations by: p. 17 Stacy Merlin; p. 23 Oxford Designers & Illustrators;
p. 24 Oxford Designers & Illustrators; p. 56 Stuart Bradford; p. 82 Greg
Paprocki; p. 87 Karen Minot; p. 94 Karen Minot.

*We would also like to thank the following for permission to reproduce the following
photographs:* Cover: Yongyut Kumsri/Shutterstock; Video Vocabulary (used
throughout the book): Oleksiy Mark/Shutterstock; p. 2 Kemal Taner/
Shutterstock; p. 4 Nico Kai/Getty Images (Boy in restaurant),
lightwavemedia/Shutterstock (Girl smiling), Anthony Hatley/Alamy (Boy
studying); p. 6 Relaximages/Alamy (Boy reading), Blend Images - Jose Luis
Pelaez Inc/Getty Images (Man with ball), Roy Botterell/Corbis UK Ltd.
(Woman reading); p. 8 Design Pics Inc./Alamy (Businessman), Anna Peisl/
Corbis UK Ltd. (Helping elderly woman); p. 10 Adam Pretty/Getty Images;
p. 15 Image Source/Alamy; p. 16 Bruce Laurance/Getty Images; p. 17 BlueMoon
Stock/Oxford University Press; p. 20 Image Source/Corbis; p. 21 paulista/
Shutterstock, Kari Marttila/Alamy; p. 22 Serge Kozak/Corbis UK Ltd.;
p. 27 The AGE/Getty Images (Students in Germany), Michele Burgess/Alamy
(students in Kenya); p. 32 Sam Bloomberg-Rissman/Getty Images; p. 36 the
food passionates/Corbis; p. 37 mama_mia/Shutterstock, Carola Koserowsky/
age fotostock/Superstock, gulfimages/Getty Images; p. 38 Laurie Rubin/
Masterfile Royalty Free (Tomatoes),Ingram/Oxford University Press
(Wedding cake), Dewitt/Shutterstock (Watermelon), Andrea Skjold/

Thinkstock (Empanadas); p. 39 Croisy/Shutterstock (Garlic), Photolibrary/
Getty Images (Herring), Cristian Baitg/Getty Images (Fruit and vegetables);
p. 40 Robert Holmes/Corbis UK Ltd. (Garlic Festival), Bon Appetit/Alamy
(Truffles), Bill Bachmann/Alamy (Herring Market), Jm Teychenne/Getty
Images (Cheese rolling); p. 46 Walter Zerla/Getty Images (Pizzas),
Razmarinka/Shutterstock (Noodle soup); p. 52 Jeremy Woodhouse/AGE
fotostock; p. 53 Dorling Kindersley/Getty Images, Pavel Vakhrushev/
Shutterstock; p. 57 Image Source Plus/Alamy; p. 59 Image Source/Getty
Images; p. 60 Dave and Les Jacobs/Getty Images; p. 61 picturesbyrob/Alamy
(Highlighter), Jeff Greenberg 2 of 6/Alamy (Storyteller); p. 62 Hill Street
Studios/Getty Images; p. 69 Harvey Silikovitz; p. 70 Image Source/Getty
Images; p. 72 Auckland; Diane/Arcaid/Corbis UK Ltd. (Japanese flat), Juice
Images/Alamy (Boy in bedroom), Corbis RF/Alamy (Family room), Lisa Marie
Thompson/Getty Images (Dining table); p. 73 Iriana Shiyan/Shutterstock;
p.77 Ben Benschneider/Seattle Times/Seattle Times (both); p. 91 David
Buffington/Blend Images/Corbis; p. 92 Marco Andras/Age Fotostock;
p. 96 David Morgan/Alamy; p. 98 Rob Lewine/Tetra Images/Corbis UK Ltd.;
p. 99 68/Ocean/Corbis UK Ltd. (Video games), Trae Patton/NBC/NBCU Photo
Bank via Getty Images/Getty Images (Biggest Loser); p. 103 Nick Hawkes/
Alamy (Messy house), Orange Line Media/Shutterstock (Man training);
p. 107 Tetra Images/Alamy; p. 108 Max Paris/Alamy; p. 112 Gunter Marx/
Gunter Marx Photography/Corbis; p. 113 Charles Mann/Getty Images, Lew
Robertson/Corbis; p. 114 Kentaroo Tryman/Getty Images; p. 115 Panoramic
Images/Getty Images; p. 116 Fedor Selivanov/Shutterstock (Zurich),
imageBROKER/Alamy (Munich), Finn Gonschior/Getty Images (Auckland);
p. 119 Johner Images/Alamy (Men shopping), Hideki Nawate/SEBUN PHOTO/
ama/Corbis UK Ltd. (Inokashira Park), 2014 Anadolu Agency/Getty Images
(Bryant Park); p. 120 Hemis/Alamy; p. 122 imageBROKER/imageBROKER/
Superstock Ltd. (Humboldt University), Westend61/Getty Images (Outdoor
markets); p. 123 olaser/Getty Images; p. 125 Shawn Hempel/Shutterstock;
p. 126 John McKenna/Alamy; p. 128 Jeff Whyte/Shutterstock; p. 129 Fraser
Hall/Getty Images; p. 135 Topic Photo Agency/AGE fotostock; p. 138 Tibor
Bognar/Alamy (village), Room to Read/Room to Read (John Wood);
p. 140 Fabio Cardoso/Corbis UK Ltd.; p. 141 Car Culture/Getty Images;
p. 142 Stephen Dunn/Getty Images; p. 143 Associated Press/Press
Association Images; p. 144 REX/Rex Features; p. 147 Visions of America/
Shutterstock; p. 149 Gene Chutka/iStockphoto; Back Cover: mozcann/
istockphoto.

SHAPING learning TOGETHER

We would like to acknowledge the teachers from all over the world who participated in the development process and review of the Q series.

Special thanks to our *Q: Skills for Success* Second Edition Topic Advisory Board

Shaker Ali Al-Mohammad, Buraimi University College, Oman; **Dr. Asmaa A. Ebrahim**, University of Sharjah, U.A.E.; **Rachel Batchilder**, College of the North Atlantic, Qatar; **Anil Bayir**, Izmir University, Turkey; **Flora Mcvay Bozkurt**, Maltepe University, Turkey; **Paul Bradley**, University of the Thai Chamber of Commerce Bangkok, Thailand; **Joan Birrell-Bertrand**, University of Manitoba, MB, Canada; **Karen E. Caldwell**, Zayed University, U.A.E.; **Nicole Hammond Carrasquel**, University of Central Florida, FL, U.S.; **Kevin Countryman**, Seneca College of Applied Arts & Technology, ON, Canada; **Julie Crocker**, Arcadia University, NS, Canada; **Marc L. Cummings**, Jefferson Community and Technical College, KY, U.S.; **Rachel DeSanto**, Hillsborough Community College Dale Mabry Campus, FL, U.S.; **Nilüfer Ertürkmen**, Ege University, Turkey; **Sue Fine**, Ras Al Khaimah Women's College (HCT), U.A.E.; **Amina Al Hashami**, Nizwa College of Applied Sciences, Oman; **Stephan Johnson**, Nagoya Shoka Daigaku, Japan; **Sean Kim**, Avalon, South Korea; **Gregory King**, Chubu Daigaku, Japan; **Seran Küçük**, Maltepe University, Turkey; **Jonee De Leon**, VUS, Vietnam; **Carol Lowther**, Palomar College, CA, U.S.; **Erin Harris-MacLeod**, St. Mary's University, NS, Canada; **Angela Nagy**, Maltepe University, Turkey; **Huynh Thi Ai Nguyen**, Vietnam; **Daniel L. Paller**, Kinjo Gakuin University, Japan; **Jangyo Parsons**, Kookmin University, South Korea; **Laila Al Qadhi**, Kuwait University, Kuwait; **Josh Rosenberger**, English Language Institute University of Montana, MT, U.S.; **Nancy Schoenfeld**, Kuwait University, Kuwait; **Jenay Seymour**, Hongik University, South Korea; **Moon-young Son**, South Korea; **Matthew Taylor**, Kinjo Gakuin Daigaku, Japan; **Burcu Tezcan-Unal**, Zayed University, U.A.E.; **Troy Tucker**, Edison State College-Lee Campus, FL, U.S.; **Kris Vicca**, Feng Chia University, Taichung; **Jisook Woo**, Incheon University, South Korea; **Dunya Yenidunya**, Ege University, Turkey

UNITED STATES Marcarena Aguilar, North Harris College, TX; Rebecca Andrade, California State University North Ridge, CA; Lesley Andrews, Boston University, MA; Deborah Anholt, Lewis and Clark College, OR; Robert Anzelde, Oakton Community College, IL; Arlys Arnold, University of Minnesota, MN; Marcia Arthur, Renton Technical College, WA; Renee Ashmeade, Passaic County Community College, NJ; Anne Bachmann, Clackamas Community College, OR; Lida Baker, UCLA, CA; Ron Balsamo, Santa Rosa Junior College, CA; Lori Barkley, Portland State University, OR; Eileen Barlow, SUNY Albany, NY; Sue Bartch, Cuyahoga Community College, OH; Lora Bates, Oakton High School, VA; Barbara Batra, Nassau County Community College, NY; Nancy Baum, University of Texas at Arlington, TX; Rebecca Beck, Irvine Valley College, CA; Linda Berendsen, Oakton Community College, IL; Jennifer Binckes Lee, Howard Community College, MD; Grace Bishop, Houston Community College, TX; Jean W. Bodman, Union County College, NJ; Virginia Bouchard, George Mason University, VA; Kimberley Briesch Sumner, University of Southern California, CA; Kevin Brown, University of California, Irvine, CA; Laura Brown, Glendale Community College, CA; Britta Burton, Mission College, CA; Allison L. Callahan, Harold Washington College, IL; Gabriela Cambiasso, Harold Washington College, IL; Jackie Campbell, Capistrano Unified School District, CA; Adele C. Camus, George Mason University, VA; Laura Chason, Savannah College, GA; Kerry Linder Catana, Language Studies International, NY; An Cheng, Oklahoma State University, OK; Carole Collins, North Hampton Community College, PA; Betty R. Compton, Intercultural Communications College, HI; Pamela Couch, Boston University, MA; Fernanda Crowe, Intrax International Institute, CA; Vicki Curtis, Santa Cruz, CA; Margo Czinski, Washtenaw Community College, MI; David Dahnke, Lone Star College, TX; Gillian M. Dale, CA; L. Dalgish, Concordia College, MN; Christopher Davis, John Jay College, NY; Sherry Davis, Irvine University, CA; Natalia de Cuba, Nassau County Community College, NY; Sonia Delgadillo, Sierra College, CA; Esmeralda Diriye, Cypress College & Cal Poly, CA; Marta O. Dmytrenko-Ahrabian, Wayne State University, MI; Javier Dominguez, Central High School, SC; Jo Ellen Downey-Greer, Lansing Community College, MI; Jennifer Duclos, Boston University, MA; Yvonne Duncan, City College of San Francisco, CA; Paul Dydman, USC Language Academy, CA; Anna Eddy, University of Michigan-Flint, MI; Zohan El-Gamal, Glendale Community College, CA; Jennie Farnell, University of Connecticut, CT; Susan Fedors, Howard Community College, MD; Valerie Fiechter, Mission College, CA; Ashley Fifer, Nassau County Community College, NY; Matthew Florence, Intrax International Institute, CA; Kathleen Flynn, Glendale College, CA; Elizabeth Fonsea, Nassau County Community College, NY; Eve Fonseca, St. Louis Community College, MO; Elizabeth Foss, Washtenaw Community College, MI; Duff C. Galda, Pima Community College, AZ; Christiane Galvani, Houston Community College, TX; Gretchen Gerber, Howard Community College, MD; Ray Gonzalez, Montgomery College, MD; Janet Goodwin, University of California, Los Angeles, CA; Alyona Gorokhova, Grossmont College, CA; John Graney, Santa Fe College, FL; Kathleen Green, Central High School, AZ; Nancy Hamadou, Pima Community College-West Campus, AZ; Webb

Hamilton, De Anza College, San Jose City College, CA; Janet Harclerode, Santa Monica Community College, CA; Sandra Hartmann, Language and Culture Center, TX; Kathy Haven, Mission College, CA; Roberta Hendrick, Cuyahoga Community College, OH; Ginny Heringer, Pasadena City College, CA; Adam Henricksen, University of Maryland, MD; Carolyn Ho, Lone Star College-CyFair, TX; Peter Hoffman, LaGuardia Community College, NY; Linda Holden, College of Lake County, IL; Jana Holt, Lake Washington Technical College, WA; Antonio Iccarino, Boston University, MA; Gail Ibele, University of Wisconsin, WI; Nina Ito, American Language Institute, CSU Long Beach, CA; Linda Jensen, UCLA, CA; Lisa Jurkowitz, Pima Community College, CA; Mandy Kama, Georgetown University, Washington, DC; Stephanie Kasuboski, Cuyahoga Community College, OH; Chigusa Katoku, Mission College, CA; Sandra Kawamura, Sacramento City College, CA; Gail Kellersberger, University of Houston-Downtown, TX; Jane Kelly, Durham Technical Community College, NC; Maryanne Kildare, Nassau County Community College, NY; Julie Park Kim, George Mason University, VA; Kindra Kinyon, Los Angeles Trade-Technical College, CA; Matt Kline, El Camino College, CA; Lisa Kovacs-Morgan, University of California, San Diego, CA; Claudia Kupiec, DePaul University, IL; Renee La Rue, Lone Star College-Montgomery, TX; Janet Langon, Glendale College, CA; Lawrence Lawson, Palomar College, CA; Rachele Lawton, The Community College of Baltimore County, MD; Alice Lee, Richland College, TX; Esther S. Lee, CSUF & Mt. SAC, CA; Cherie Lenz-Hackett, University of Washington, WA; Joy Leventhal, Cuyahoga Community College, OH; Alice Lin, UCI Extension, CA; Monica Lopez, Cerritos College, CA; Dustin Lovell, FLS International Marymount College, CA; Carol Lowther, Palomar College, CA; Candace Lynch-Thompson, North Orange County Community College District, CA; Thi Thi Ma, City College of San Francisco, CA; Steve Mac Isaac, USC Long Academy, CA; Denise Maduli-Williams, City College of San Francisco, CA; Eileen Mahoney, Camelback High School, AZ; Naomi Mardock, MCC-Omaha, NE; Brigitte Maronde, Harold Washington College, IL; Marilyn Marquis, Laposita College CA; Doris Martin, Glendale Community College; Pasadena City College, CA; Keith Maurice, University of Texas at Arlington, TX; Nancy Mayer, University of Missouri-St. Louis, MO; Aziah McNamara, Kansas State University, KS; Billie McQuillan, Education Heights, MN; Karen Merritt, Glendale Union High School District, AZ; Holly Milkowart, Johnson County Community College, KS; Eric Moyer, Intrax International Institute, CA; Gino Muzzatti, Santa Rosa Junior College, CA; Sandra Navarro, Glendale Community College, CA; Than Nyeinkhin, ELAC, PCC, CA; William Nedrow, Triton College, IL; Eric Nelson, University of Minnesota, MN; Than Nyeinkhin, ELAC, PCC, CA; Fernanda Ortiz, Center for English as a Second Language at the University of Arizona, AZ; Rhony Ory, Ygnacio Valley High School, CA; Paul Parent, Montgomery College, MD; Dr. Sumeeta Patnaik, Marshall University, WV; Oscar Pedroso, Miami Dade College, FL; Robin Persiani, Sierra College, CA; Patricia Prenz-Belkin, Hostos Community College, NY; Suzanne Powell, University of Louisville, KY; Jim Ranalli, Iowa State University, IA; Toni R. Randall, Santa Monica College, CA; Vidya Rangachari, Mission College, CA; Elizabeth Rasmussen, Northern Virginia Community College, VA; Lara Ravitch, Truman College, IL;

Industry, Vietnam; **Do Thi Thanh Nhan**, Hanoi University, Vietnam; **Dale Kazuo Nishi**, Aoyama English Conversation School, Japan; **Huynh Thi Ai Nguyen**, Vietnam; **Dongshin Oh**, YBM PLS, South Korea; **Keiko Okada**, Dokkyo Daigaku, Japan; **Louise Ohashi**, Shukutoku University, Japan; **Yongjun Park**, Sangji University, South Korea; **Donald Patnaude**, Ajarn Donald's English Language Services, Thailand; **Virginia Peng**, Ritsumeikan University, Japan; **Suangkanok Piboonthamnont**, Rajamangala University of Technology, Thailand; **Simon Pitcher**, Business English Teaching Services, Japan; **John C. Probert**, New Education Worldwide, Thailand; **Do Thi Hoa Quyen**, Ton Duc Thang University, Vietnam; **John P. Racine**, Dokkyo University, Japan; **Kevin Ramsden**, Kyoto University of Foreign Studies, Japan; **Luis Rappaport**, Cung Thieu Nha Ha Noi, Vietnam; **Lisa Reshad**, Konan Daigaku Hyogo, Japan; **Peter Riley**, Taisho University, Japan; **Thomas N. Robb**, Kyoto Sangyo University, Japan; **Rory Rosszell**, Meiji Daigaku, Japan; **Maria Feti Rosyani**, Universitas Kristen Indonesia, Indonesia; **Greg Rouault**, Konan University, Japan; **Chris Ruddenklau**, Kindai University, Japan; **Hans-Gustav Schwartz**, Thailand; **Mary-Jane Scott**, Soongsil University, South Korea; **Dara Sheahan**, Seoul National University, South Korea; **James Sherlock**, A.P.W. Angthong, Thailand; **Prof. Shieh**, Minghsin University of Science & Technology, Xinfeng; **Yuko Shimizu**, Ritsumeikan University, Japan; **Suzila Mohd Shukor**, Universiti Sains Malaysia, Malaysia; **Stephen E. Smith**, Mahidol University, Thailand; **Moon-young Son**, South Korea; **Seunghee Son**, Anyang University, South Korea; **Mi-young Song**, Kyungwon University, South Korea; **Lisa Sood**, VUS, BIS, Vietnam; **Jason Stewart**, Taejon International Language School, South Korea; **Brian A. Stokes**, Korea University, South Korea; **Mulder Su**, Shih-Chien University, Kaohsiung; **Yoomi Suh**, English Plus, South Korea; **Yun-Fang Sun**, Wenzao Ursuline College of Languages, Kaohsiung; **Richard Swingle**, Kansai Gaidai University, Japan; **Sanford Taborn**, Kinjo Gakuin Daigaku, Japan; **Mamoru Takahashi**, Akita Prefectural University, Japan; **Tran Hoang Tan**, School of International Training, Vietnam; **Takako Tanaka**, Doshisha University, Japan; **Jeffrey Taschner**, American University Alumni Language Center, Thailand; **Matthew Taylor**, Kinjo Gakuin Daigaku, Japan; **Michael Taylor**, International Pioneers School, Thailand; **Kampanart Thammaphati**, Wattana Wittaya Academy, Thailand; **Tran Duong The**, Sao Mai Language Center, Vietnam; **Tran Dinh Tho**, Duc Tri Secondary School, Vietnam; **Huynh Thi Anh Thu**, Nhatrang College of Culture Arts and Tourism, Vietnam; **Peter Timmins**, Peter's English School, Japan; **Fumie Togano**, Hosei Daini High School, Japan; **F. Sigmund Topor**, Keio University Language School, Japan; **Tu Trieu**, Rise VN, Vietnam; **Yen-Cheng Tseng**, Chang-Jung Christian University, Tainan; **Pei-Hsuan Tu**, National Cheng Kung University, Tainan City; **Hajime Uematsu**, Hirosaki University, Japan; **Rachel Um**, Mok-dong Oedae English School, South Korea; **David Underhill**, EEExpress, Japan; **Ben Underwood**, Kugenuma High School, Japan; **Siriluck Usaha**, Sripatum University, Thailand; **Tyas Budi Utami**, Indonesia; **Nguyen Thi Van**, Far East International School, Vietnam; **Stephan Van Eycken**, Kosei Gakuen Girls High School, Japan; **Zisa Velasquez**, Taihu International School/Semarang International School, China/Indonesia; **Jeffery Walter**, Sangji University, South Korea; **Bill White**, Kinki University, Japan; **Yohanes De Deo Widyastoko**, Xaverius Senior High School, Indonesia; **Dylan Williams**, SNU, South Korea; **Jisuk Woo**, Ichean University, South Korea; **Greg Chung-Hsien Wu**, Providence University, Taichung; **Xun Xiaoming**, BLCU, China; **Hui-Lien Yeh**, Chai Nan University of Pharmacy and Science, Tainan; **Sittiporn Yodnil**, Huachiew Chalermprakiet University, Thailand; **Shamshul Helmy Zambahari**, Universiti Teknologi Malaysia, Malaysia; **Ming-Yuli**, Chang Jung Christian University, Tainan; **Aimin Fadhlee bin Mahmud Zuhodi**, Kuala Terengganu Science School, Malaysia;

TURKEY **Shirley F. Akis**, American Culture Association/Fomara; **Gül Akkoç**, Boğaziçi University; **Seval Akmeşe**, Haliç University; **Ayşenur Akyol**, Ege University; **Ayşe Umut Arıbaş**, Beykent University; **Gökhan Asan**, Kapadokya Vocational College; **Hakan Asan**, Kapadokya Vocational College; **Julia Asan**, Kapadokya Vocational College; **Azarvan Atac**, Piri Reis University; **Nur Babat**, Kapadokya Vocational College; **Feyza Balakbabalar**, Kadir Has University; **Gözde Balıkçi**, Beykent University; **Deniz Balım**, Haliç University; **Asli Başdoğan**, Kadir Has University; **Ayla Bayram**, Kapadokya Vocational College; **Pinar Bilgiç**, Kadir Has University; **Kenan Bozkurt**, Kapadokya Vocational College; **Yonca Bozkurt**, Ege University; **Frank Carr**, Piri Reis; **Mengü Noyan Çengel**, Ege University; **Elif Doğan**, Ege University; **Natalia Donmez**, 29 Mayıs Üniverste; **Nalan Emirsoy**, Kadir Has University; **Ayşe Engin**, Kadir Has University; **Ayhan Gedikbaş**, Ege University; **Gülşah Gençer**, Beykent University; **Seyit Ömer Gök**, Gediz University; **Tuğba Gök**, Gediz University; **İlkay Gökçe**, Ege University; **Zeynep Birinci Guler**, Maltepe University; **Neslihan Güler**, Kadir Has University; **Sircan Gümüş**,

Kadir Has University; **Nesrin Gündoğu**, T.C. Piri Reis University; **Tanju Gurpinar**, Piri Reis University; **Selin Gurturk**, Piri Reis University; **Neslihan Gurutku**, Piri Reis University; **Roger Hewitt**, Maltepe University; **Nilüfer İbrahimoğlu**, Beykent University; **Nevin Kaftelen**, Kadir Has University; **Sultan Kalin**, Kapadokya Vocational College; **Sema Kaplan Karabina**, Anadolu University; **Eray Kara**, Giresun University; **Beylü Karayazgan**, Ege University; **Darren Kelso**, Piri Reis University; **Trudy Kittle**, Kapadokya Vocational College; **Şaziye Konaç**, Kadir Has University; **Güneş Korkmaz**, Kapadokya Vocational College; **Robert Ledbury**, Izmir University of Economics; **Ashley Lucas**, Maltepe University; **Bülent Nedium Uça**, Dogus University; **Murat Nurlu**, Ege University; **Mollie Owens**, Kadir Has University; **Oya Özağaç**, Boğaziçi University; **Funda Özcan**, Ege University; **İlkay Özdemir**, Ege University; **Ülkü Öztürk**, Gediz University; **Cassondra Puls**, Anadolu University; **Yelda Sarikaya**, Cappadocia Vocational College; **Müge Şekercioğlu**, Ege University; **Melis Senol**, Canakkale Onsekiz Mart University, The School of Foreign Languages; **Patricia Sümer**, Kadir Has University; **Rex Surface**, Beykent University; **Mustafa Torun**, Kapadokya Vocational College; **Tansel Üstünloğlu**, Ege University; **Fatih Yücel**, Beykent University; **Şule Yüksel**, Ege University;

THE MIDDLE EAST **Amina Saif Mohammed Al Hashamia**, Nizwa College of Applied Sciences, Oman; **Jennifer Baran**, Kuwait University, Kuwait; **Phillip Chappells**, GEMS Modern Academy, U.A.E.; **Sharon Ruth Devaneson**, Ibri College of Technology, Oman; **Hanaa El-Deeb**, Canadian International College, Egypt; **Yvonne Eaton**, Community College of Qatar, Qatar; **Brian Gay**, Sultan Qaboos University, Oman; **Gail Al Hafidh**, Sharjah Women's College (HCT), U.A.E.; **Jonathan Hastings**, American Language Center, Jordan; **Laurie Susan Hilu**, English Language Centre, University of Bahrain, Bahrain; **Abraham Irannezhad**, Mehre Aval, Iran; **Kevin Kempe**, CNA-Q, Qatar; **Jill Newby James**, University of Nizwa; **Mary Kay Klein**, American University of Sharjah, U.A.E.; **Sian Khoury**, Fujairah Women's College (HCT), U.A.E.; **Hussein Dehghan Manshadi**, Farhang Pajooh & Jaam-e-Jam Language School, Iran; **Jessica March**, American University of Sharjah, U.A.E.; **Neil McBeath**, Sultan Qaboos University, Oman; **Sandy McDonagh**, Abu Dhabi Men's College (HCT), U.A.E.; **Rob Miles**, Sharjah Women's College (HCT), U.A.E.; **Michael Kevin Neumann**, Al Ain Men's College (HCT), U.A.E.;

LATIN AMERICA **Aldana Aguirre**, Argentina; **Claudia Almeida**, Coordenação de Idiomas, Brazil; **Cláudia Arias**, Brazil; **Maria de los Angeles Barba**, FES Acatlan UNAM, Mexico; **Lilia Barrios**, Universidad Autónoma de Tamaulipas, Mexico; **Adán Beristain**, UAEM, Mexico; **Ricardo Böck**, Manoel Ribas, Brazil; **Edson Braga**, CNA, Brazil; **Marli Buttelli**, Mater et Magistra, Brazil; **Alessandra Campos**, Inova Centro de Linguas, Brazil; **Priscila Catta Preta Ribeiro**, Brazil; **Gustavo Cestari**, Access International School, Brazil; **Walter D'Alessandro**, Virginia Language Center, Brazil; **Lilian De Gennaro**, Argentina; **Mônica De Stefani**, Quality Centro de Idiomas, Brazil; **Julio Alejandro Flores**, BUAP, Mexico; **Mirian Freire**, CNA Vila Guilherme, Brazil; **Francisco Garcia**, Colegio Lestonnac de San Angel, Mexico; **Miriam Giovanardi**, Brazil; **Darlene Gonzalez Miy**, ITESM CCV, Mexico; **Maria Laura Grimaldi**, Argentina; **Luz Dary Guzmán**, IMPAHU, Colombia; **Carmen Koppe**, Brazil; **Monica Krutzler**, Brazil; **Marcus Murilo Lacerda**, Seven Idiomas, Brazil; **Nancy Lake**, CEL-LEP, Brazil; **Cris Lazzerini**, Brazil; **Sandra Luna**, Argentina; **Ricardo Luvisan**, Brazil; **Jorge Murilo Menezes**, ACBEU, Brazil; **Monica Navarro**, Instituto Cultural A. C., Mexico; **Joacyr Oliveira**, Faculdades Metropolitanas Unidas and Summit School for Teachers, Brazil; **Ayrton Cesar Oliveira de Araujo**, E&A English Classes, Brazil; **Ana Laura Oriente**, Seven Idiomas, Brazil; **Adelia Peña Clavel**, CELE UNAM, Mexico; **Beatriz Pereira**, Summit School, Brazil; **Miguel Perez**, Instituto Cultural, Mexico; **Cristiane Perone**, Associação Cultura Inglesa, Brazil; **Pamela Claudia Pogré**, Colegio Integral Caballito / Universidad de Flores, Argentina; **Dalva Prates**, Brazil; **Marianne Rampaso**, Iowa Idiomas, Brazil; **Daniela Rutolo**, Instituto Superior Cultural Británico, Argentina; **Maione Sampaio**, Maione Carrijo Consultoria em Inglês Ltda, Brazil; **Elaine Santesso**, TS Escola de Idiomas, Brazil; **Camila Francisco Santos**, UNS Idiomas, Brazil; **Lucia Silva**, Cooplem Idiomas, Brazil; **Maria Adela Sorzio**, Instituto Superior Santa Cecilia, Argentina; **Elcio Souza**, Unibero, Brazil; **Willie Thomas**, Rainbow Idiomas, Brazil; **Sandra Villegas**, Instituto Humberto de Paolis, Argentina; **John Whelan**, La Universidad Nacional Autonoma de Mexico, Mexico

CONTENTS

UNIT 1

Social Psychology

VOCABULARY	▶	descriptive adjectives
READING	▶	identifying topics and main ideas
WRITING	▶	writing simple sentences
GRAMMAR	▶	present of *be*; simple present affirmative statements

UNIT QUESTION

What kind of person are you?

A Discuss these questions with your classmates.

1. Are you a quiet person or a noisy person? Are you tall or short? Are you funny or serious?

2. What do your friends say about you?

3. Look at the photo. Which faces look happy? Surprised? Sad? Angry? Which face is most like you?

B Listen to *The Q Classroom* online. Then answer these questions.

1. Which speaker is a good student? Which one does not talk a lot? Which one likes to go out? Which one is a serious person?

2. Which student is most like you? Why?

 C Go to the Online Discussion Board to discuss the Unit Question with your classmates.

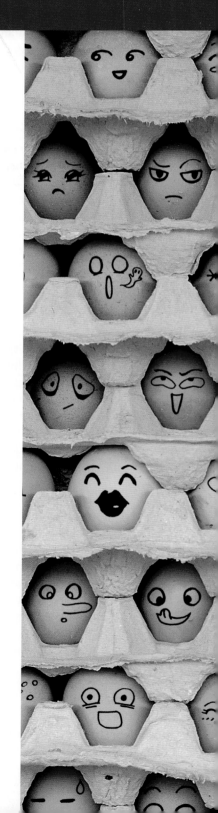

UNIT ▶▶▶ OBJECTIVE

Read a magazine article. Find information and ideas to write about your personality, appearance, and interests.

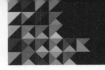

READING | ## What Kind of Person Are You?

 **UNIT OBJECTIVE** ▶▶▶ You are going to read a magazine article about different kinds of people. Use the article to find information and ideas for your Unit Assignment.

PREVIEW THE READING

A. **VOCABULARY** Here are some words from the reading. Read the sentences. Circle the correct explanation.

Sam is outgoing.

Amy is fashionable.

Jack is messy.

1. Please <u>describe</u> your brother. Is he tall? What color is his hair?
   a. Help your brother.
   b. Tell me about your brother.

2. Sam is very <u>outgoing</u>. He likes to meet new people.
   a. Sam is friendly.
   b. Sam is quiet.

3. Soraya is very <u>talkative</u>. She speaks to everyone.
   a. Soraya talks a lot.
   b. Soraya talks very little.

4. Nawaf has a nice <u>personality</u>. He's very kind and helpful.
   a. Nawaf acts in a nice way.
   b. Nawaf has a nice name.

5. Amy is very <u>fashionable</u>. She always wears new clothes.
   a. Amy doesn't care about clothes.
   b. Amy likes clothes, and she dresses well.

🔑 Oxford 2000 keywords

6. Jack's room is <u>messy</u>. There are books and papers everywhere.
   a. Jack's room is clean.
   b. Jack's room is not clean.

7. Toshi is not very tall and not very short. He is <u>average</u> height.
   a. Toshi's height is like most people.
   b. Toshi's height is not like most people.

8. John is a <u>serious</u> person. He almost never laughs.
   a. John is happy, and he's a funny person.
   b. John is quiet, and he's not funny.

B. Complete the sentences with the words from Activity A. (You will not use all the words.)

1. I'm not thin and I'm not heavy. My weight is about _____.

2. Can you _____ your father? What does he look like?

3. My boots are ten years old. They aren't very _____.

4. She is a(n) _____ person. She talks to everyone.

5. Mary is shy. She has a quiet _____.

6. Don't be _____ all the time. Have some fun!

iQ ONLINE **C. Go online for more practice with the vocabulary.**

Tip for Success

Before you read a text, look at the title. Then look at the pictures. What do they tell you about the reading?

D. PREVIEW This magazine article describes different kinds of people. Look at the photos in the article. Write one word to describe each person.

1. Carlos is _____.

2. Rob is _____.

3. Sarah is _____.

E. QUICK WRITE Describe yourself. Answer these questions. Use this section for your Unit Assignment.

1. What do you look like? _____

2. What do you like to do? _____

3. What is your personality like? _____

WORK WITH THE READING

A. Read the magazine article. Find information about different kinds of people.

What Kind of Person Are You?

Carlos is shy.

This week, *Talk Magazine* is asking people about themselves. Read each question and the two answers. Which answer **describes** you? Check (✓) one answer for each question.

1. **Are you a friendly person?**
   - ☐ Yes, I'm very **outgoing**. I have a lot of friends, and I like to meet new people. (*James, 18*)
   - ☐ I'm a nice guy, but I'm not very **talkative**. I have two or three good friends. I talk to them a lot. But with other people, I'm shy. (*Carlos, 23*)

2. **Are you interested in fashion?**
   - ☐ I usually wear jeans and T-shirts. I don't care about people's clothes. I'm more interested in someone's **personality**. (*Hassan, 22*)
   - ☐ Clothes are important. I like to dress well. People say I'm very **fashionable**. (*Matt, 21*)

3. **How tall are you?**
   - ☐ I'm tall—about 6 feet and 3 inches (192 centimeters). I play basketball for City University. (*Rob, 20*)
   - ☐ I have two brothers. They are both very tall—about 6 feet and 5 inches (198 centimeters)! But I'm only **average** height—about 5 feet and 9 inches (179 centimeters). (*David, 19*)

Rob is tall.

4. **Are you a neat person?**
   - ☐ I don't have time to clean. I go to school, and I also have a part-time job. I'm always busy! (*Kate, 21*)
   - ☐ I can't study in a **messy** room. I'm very busy, but I clean my room every day. (*Amanda, 18*)

5. **Are you a serious or funny person?**
   - ☐ I study a lot, so people think I'm a very **serious** person. But I also like to have fun. (*Sarah, 21*)
   - ☐ I love to laugh and tell jokes. (*Emma, 24*)

6. **What is your best subject in school?**
   - ☐ I'm good at math. It's my favorite subject. For some people, math is hard. For me, it is easy. (*Khalid, 18*)
   - ☐ My best subjects are English and French. I also speak Spanish! (*Pablo, 17*)

Sarah is serious.

B. Read the statements. Write *T* (true) or *F* (false). Then correct each false statement to make it true.

____ 1. James likes to meet new people.

____ 2. Carlos is very talkative.

____ 3. Hassan is fashionable.

____ 4. David is tall.

____ 5. Kate is a very neat person.

____ 6. Amanda's room is messy.

____ 7. Sarah studies very hard.

____ 8. Emma is a very serious person.

____ 9. Math is easy for Khalid.

____ 10. Pablo is good at English.

C. Match the person's name with the description.

____ 1. Hassan   a. is shy with other people

____ 2. Kate   b. doesn't care about clothes

____ 3. Khalid   c. plays basketball

____ 4. Rob   d. is about average height

____ 5. Carlos   e. doesn't have time to clean

____ 6. Pablo   f. studies a lot

____ 7. Emma   g. likes to tell jokes

____ 8. David   h. likes math

____ 9. Sarah   i. speaks French and Spanish

D. Complete each sentence with words from the box.

average	funny	neat	personality	speaks
fashionable	messy	outgoing	serious	subject

1. Amanda is a _____ person.

2. James is very _____ .

3. Math is Khalid's favorite _____ .

4. Pablo _____ Spanish.

5. People say that Matt is _____.

6. Hassan is interested in a person's _____.

7. People think Sarah is a _____ person.

8. David is _____ height.

9. Emma is _____.

10. Kate's room is _____.

 E. Go online to read *Olympic Skater Kim Yuna* and check your comprehension.

Building Vocabulary | Descriptive adjectives

We use **adjectives** to describe people.

Adjectives for appearance	Adjectives for personality
Height: tall, short, average height **Weight:** heavy, thin, average weight **Hair:** blond, brown, red, black	kind, friendly, helpful, nice, generous shy, quiet smart, intelligent funny, serious

generous

helpful

A. Complete the sentences. Circle the correct answer.

1. He's (tall / thin / kind) because he doesn't eat a lot.

2. Talal reads a lot of books. He is very (intelligent / blond / outgoing).

3. I laughed because he is a (nice / friendly / funny) guy.

4. Aldo doesn't talk much. He is (short / helpful / shy).

5. Sultan is a good basketball player because he is (generous / tall / blond).

6. Thank you very much. You are very (helpful / quiet / heavy).

7. This class is easy for her. She is (funny / smart / shy).

8. Rick shares money with other people. He is (generous / serious / thin).

B. Match the words with their opposites.

1. outgoing ____   a. neat

2. tall ____   b. serious

3. messy ____   c. shy

4. heavy ____   d. talkative

5. funny ____   e. short

6. quiet ____   f. thin

C. What other words describe people? Write them in the chart. Then write five sentences using the words.

Words to describe appearance	Words to describe personality

 D. Go online for more practice with descriptive adjectives.

Reading Skill | Identifying topics and main ideas

Every paragraph has a **topic** and a **main idea**.

1. **The topic** Usually, you can say the topic in one or two words. To identify the topic, ask this question: *What is this paragraph about?*

   In this paragraph, the topic is "**my brother**." The topic <u>repeats</u> in the paragraph.

   > <u>My brother</u>, Miteb, is very popular. Everyone likes <u>him</u>. Why? For one thing, <u>he</u> is very outgoing. <u>He</u> laughs a lot, and <u>he</u> tells jokes. <u>He</u> makes people happy. For these reasons, <u>my brother</u> has a lot of friends.

2. **The main idea** Usually, you can say the main idea in a short sentence. To identify the main idea, ask this question: *What is the most important idea in this paragraph?*

   In the paragraph above, the main idea is "**My brother, Miteb, is very popular**." The other sentences in the paragraph explain this idea.

 **Tip for Success**

The main idea is often in the first or last sentence in a paragraph, but not always.

A. Read the article. Then answer the questions on page 11.

Cristiano Ronaldo

1   Cristiano Ronaldo is a famous soccer player. He is from Portugal. He plays for a soccer team in Spain. The team is called Real Madrid.

2   Ronaldo is good at soccer. In his free time, he is also interested in business. He owns two clothing stores in Portugal. One store is in Lisbon, and one is in Madeira.

3   Each year, his team pays him $28 million. Companies also pay him to wear their clothes and shoes. Cristiano Ronaldo is a rich man.

4   Ronaldo is also very generous. He uses his money to help people around the world. Sometimes he gives his money to people after a flood or an earthquake. He is a nice guy!

1. What is the topic of the reading? _____

2. What is the main idea of paragraph 1?
   a. Ronaldo is a famous soccer player.
   b. His team is called Real Madrid.

3. What is the main idea of paragraph 2?
   a. One store is in Lisbon.
   b. Ronaldo is interested in business.

4. What is the main idea of paragraph 3?
   a. Companies pay Ronaldo to wear their clothes.
   b. Ronaldo is a rich man.

5. What is the main idea of paragraph 4?
   a. Ronaldo is a serious person.
   b. He gives his money to people.

 **B. Go online** for more practice with identifying topics and main ideas.

 WRITE WHAT YOU THINK

A. Take this magazine survey.

Who are you?
Which words describe you? Check (✓) your answers.

☐ tall	☐ serious	☐ quiet
☐ short	☐ nice	☐ outgoing
☐ intelligent	☐ smart	☐ funny
☐ thin	☐ shy	☐ helpful
☐ kind	☐ friendly	☐ neat
☐ fashionable	☐ talkative	☐ messy

B. **Complete these tasks with a partner. Look back at your Quick Write on page 5. Think about what you learned.**

1. List three words to describe both you and your partner.

   _____   _____   _____

2. Ask your partner, "What are you interested in? What are you good at?" Write your partner's answers.

   My partner is good at…   *My partner is interested in…*

   _____

   _____

   _____

C. **Go online to watch the video about risk takers. Then check your comprehension.**

> **VIDEO VOCABULARY**
>
> **danger** *(n.)* the possibility that something bad may happen
> **fully-formed** *(adj.)* completely grown
> **taking risks** *(idm.)* doing something dangerous
> **teenager** *(n.)* a person who is 13 to 19 years old

D. **Think about the unit video and the reading as you discuss these questions. Then choose one question and write an answer.**

1. Who is your best friend? Describe him or her. What does he or she look like? What is his or her personality like?

2. Does your best friend like to take risks?

Question: _____

My answer: _____

   _____

   _____

   _____

WRITING

UNIT OBJECTIVE ▶▶▶
At the end of this unit, you are going to write about your personality, appearance, and interests. Your sentences will include information from the reading, the unit video, and your own ideas.

Writing Skill   Writing simple sentences

Subjects and verbs

A sentence in English needs a **subject**. The subject performs the action. Usually the subject comes at the beginning of the sentence. The subject is a noun or a pronoun.

Tom goes to school.
Dana likes basketball.
She is good at math.

A sentence can have more than one subject. Use the word *and* with two subjects.

Ahmed **and** Salim are from Oman.   John **and** Mary enjoy sports.

A sentence also needs a **verb**. The verb is a word that describes the action.

Asako **eats** lunch every day.
Cristiano Ronaldo **plays** soccer.
The students **relax** on their vacation.

Writing **Tip**

When you write, be sure that every sentence has a subject and a verb.

A. Underline the subjects. **Circle** the verbs.

1. David is tall.

2. I usually wear jeans and T-shirts.

3. Sarah studies very hard.

4. Steve is very funny.

5. Nat likes soccer.

6. Liz enjoys new clothes.

B. Put the words in the correct order.

1. likes / television / Pablo _____.

2. English / studies / Maria _____.

3. many books / Fatima / reads _____.

4. cleans / her room / Emma _____.

5. very outgoing / are / Ken and Hiroki _____.

iQ ONLINE   **C. Go online for more practice with simple sentences.**

Present of *be*

Use the verb *be* to identify and describe people and things.

subject		*be*	(not)	
I		**am**		a student.
You / We / They		**are**	**(not)**	tall.
He / She / It		**is**		from Portugal.

- A **contraction** makes two words into one word. It has an apostrophe (').

I am = I'm	He is = He's
You are = You're	She is = She's
They are = They're	It is = It's

- There are two negative contractions for *are not*.

're not	aren't
They**'re not** short.	You **aren't** tall.

- There are two negative contractions for *is not*.

's not	isn't
She**'s not** American.	He **isn't** from England.

Asking questions				Answers
wh- word	*be*	subject		
Who	**is**	Fahad's friend?		Sam **is** Fahad's friend.
What	**are**	his interests?		His interests **are** soccer and travel.
Where	**are**		you from?	I **am** from Saudi Arabia.

A. Complete the paragraph with *am*, *is*, **or** *are*.

My name _____is_____ Jacob. I _____ from
Canada. I _____ tall and my hair _____
very short. Right now, I _____ a student in Mexico.
I _____ interested in science. My school _____

Jacob

for international students. The students _____ from all
over the world. I _____ shy, but it _____ easy
to make friends at my school. My classmates _____ very
friendly. Sometimes they _____ serious, too.

B. **Complete the sentences. Use the correct positive or negative form of**
_be_. Use contractions.

1. John _____isn't_____ heavy. He weighs only 120 pounds (54 kilos).

2. You talk a lot. You _____ quiet.

3. I'm not Canadian. I _____ from Kuwait.

4. I _____ shy. I am outgoing.

5. They _____ good at basketball because they're very short.

6. She _____ a student. She's a teacher.

Tip for Success

A question ends with
a question mark (?).

C. **Put the words in the correct order to make questions. Then answer**
the questions.

1. who / teacher / your / is _____

_____

2. interests / what / your / are _____

_____

3. you / are / what / at / good _____

_____

4. are / you / where / from _____

_____

5. your / when / is / exam _____

_____

Simple present

The simple present describes habits, facts, or feelings.

> Rasha **eats** breakfast every morning.   Sarah **feels** happy today.
> Matt **goes** to Brown University.   Rob **likes** to cook.

Affirmative statements

subject	verb	
I / You / We / They	**come**	from Australia.
He / She / It	**comes**	

Use the base verb + -*s* or -*es* after *he*, *she*, and *it*.

Add -*s* after most verbs	get**s**, like**s**, listen**s**, play**s**
Add -*es* after -*ch*, -*sh*, or -*o*.	doe**s**, goe**s**, wash**es**, watch**es**
If the verb ends in a consonant + -*y*, change the *y* to *i* and add -*es*.	cr**ies**, fl**ies**, stud**ies**, tr**ies**
Irregular third-person form	have → **has**

D. Complete the sentences. Use the correct form of the verbs.

go	have	read	study	take	wash	watch

Claire

1. They _____ TV every night at 8:00.

2. Matt _____ to school every day.

3. Rob _____ his car every weekend. It's a very clean car!

4. Claire _____ the newspaper every day.

5. We _____ a trip every summer.

6. I _____ brown hair.

7. He _____ in the library in the afternoons.

iQ ONLINE   **E.** Go online for more practice with the present of *be* and simple present affirmative statements.

F. Go online for the grammar expansion.

UNIT OBJECTIVE ▶▶▶ In this assignment, you are going to write about your personality, appearance, and interests. Think about the Unit Question, "What kind of person are you?" Use the reading, the unit video, and your work in this unit. Look at the Self-Assessment checklist on page 18.

iQ ONLINE Go to the Online Writing Tutor for a writing model and alternate Unit Assignments.

A. **BRAINSTORM** Read the information about Lauren. Rewrite each sentence. Make it true for you. Change the words or use *not*.

I am from China. I am not from England.

Lauren Baker

My appearance and background

I am from England.
I am twenty years old.
My hair is blond.
I'm about average height.

My personality

I am very outgoing.
I like new people.

My interests

I enjoy reading and school.
I like clothes and fashion.
I am interested in science and history.
I am good at sports and English.

B. WRITE Use your **BRAINSTORM** sentences to answer these questions about yourself. Write two sentences for each question. Go to *iQ Online* to use the Online Writing Tutor.

1. a. What do you look like?
   b. What are you like? Describe your personality.
   c. What are you interested in?
   d. What are you good at?

2. Use descriptive adjectives to add more information.

C. REVISE Review your sentences with a partner. Read your partner's sentences. Then go online and use the Peer Review worksheet. Discuss the review with your partner.

D. EDIT AND REWRITE Complete the Self-Assessment checklist. Make final changes to your sentences. Be prepared to hand in your work or discuss it in class.

Yes	No	SELF-ASSESSMENT
☐	☐	Do you use descriptive adjectives?
☐	☐	Does every sentence have a subject and a verb?
☐	☐	Do you use the present of *be* correctly?
☐	☐	Do you use contractions correctly?
☐	☐	Do you use the simple present correctly in affirmative statements?
☐	☐	Do you use vocabulary from the unit?

E. REFLECT Go to the Online Discussion Board to discuss these questions.

1. What is something new you learned in this unit?

2. Look back at the Unit Question—What kind of person are you? Is your answer different now than when you started the unit? If yes, how is it different?

TRACK YOUR SUCCESS

Circle the words and phrases you have learned in this unit.

Nouns
height 🔑
personality 🔑
subject 🔑
weight 🔑

Verbs
describe 🔑
speak 🔑

Adjectives
average 🔑
blond
busy 🔑
fashionable 🔑

friendly 🔑
funny 🔑
generous 🔑
heavy 🔑
helpful 🔑
intelligent 🔑 AWL
kind 🔑
messy 🔑
neat 🔑
nice 🔑
noisy 🔑
outgoing
quiet 🔑

serious 🔑
short 🔑
shy 🔑
smart
talkative
tall 🔑
thin 🔑

Phrases
be good at
be interested in

🔑 Oxford 2000 keywords
AWL Academic Word List

Check (✓) the skills you learned. If you need more work on a skill, refer to the page(s) in parentheses.

VOCABULARY ■	I can use descriptive adjectives. (p. 8)
READING ■	I can identify topics and main ideas. (p. 10)
WRITING ■	I can write simple sentences. (p. 13)
GRAMMAR ■	I can use the present of *be* and simple present affirmative statements. (pp. 14–16)
UNIT OBJECTIVE ▶▶▶ ■	I can find information and ideas to write about my personality, appearance, and interests.

VOCABULARY	▶	word families
READING	▶	scanning for names, dates, and times
WRITING	▶	capitalization and punctuation
GRAMMAR	▶	simple present

UNIT QUESTION

Do students spend too much time in school?

A Work with a partner. Complete these statements about students. Then discuss your ideas with your classmates.

1. Students spend about _____ hours in school each day.

2. Students spend about _____ hours doing homework each day.

3. Students spend about _____ months in school each year.

B Listen to *The Q Classroom* online. Then answer these questions.

1. How does each person—Yuna, Felix, Marcus, and Sophy—answer the Unit Question?

2. Do you agree with Sophy about how much time students spend in school? Why or why not?

iQ ONLINE **C** Go online to watch the video about school vacations. Then check your comprehension.

VIDEO VOCABULARY

agree *(v.)* to have the same opinion as another person

disagree *(v.)* to have a different opinion from someone else

habit *(n.)* something that you do very often

relax *(v.)* to rest and be calm; to become less worried

routine *(n.)* your usual way of doing things

iQ ONLINE **D** Go to the Online Discussion Board to discuss the Unit Question with your classmates.

21

READING | Comparing Schools in Three Countries

You are going to read a magazine article about schools in different countries. Use the article to find information and ideas for your Unit Assignment.

PREVIEW THE READING

Vocabulary Skill Review

As you learn new vocabulary, pay attention to descriptive adjectives. For example, some descriptive adjectives to use with the noun *class* are *easy, difficult, interesting, boring, first,* and *last.*

A. VOCABULARY Here are some words from the reading. Read the sentences. Circle what the <u>underlined</u> words mean.

1. My classmates study during the <u>academic</u> year.
   a. school   b. summer

2. Students <u>attend</u> school for seven hours every day.
   a. leave   b. go to

3. I take a one-hour <u>break</u> at lunch time.
   a. rest   b. exercise

4. The class <u>lasts</u> from 9:00 to 10:00.
   a. begins   b. starts and ends

5. During <u>study period</u>, students do homework or read.
   a. special study time   b. discussion time

6. There are three <u>terms</u> in the school year: fall, winter, and spring.
   a. time periods   b. months

7. Some students wear <u>uniforms</u> to school. Everyone dresses the same.
   a. backpacks   b. special clothing

8. My family usually goes to the beach for summer <u>vacation</u>.
   a. holiday time   b. winter time

🔑 Oxford 2000 keywords

B. Go online for more practice with the vocabulary.

C. **PREVIEW** Look at the title of the magazine article and the maps. What three countries will the article be about?

Tip for Success

The word *school* can refer to any educational institute. The words *college* and *university* often have the same meaning.

D. **QUICK WRITE** Think about your school. Answer these questions. Use this section for your Unit Assignment.

1. How long is the school day? _____

2. How long is the school year? _____

3. When do students have vacation? _____

WORK WITH THE READING

A. Read the magazine article and find information about education in different countries.

Comparing Schools in Three Countries

1   Do students spend too much time in school? We asked some students to share their ideas about school in their countries.

don't go to school on Wednesday afternoon, but we **attend** school on Saturday morning. School on Saturday morning isn't very fun!"

France

Kenya

2   Marie lives in France. She says, "My school year **lasts** from August to June with four seven-week **terms**. We have one or two weeks of **vacation** after each term, and we have a two-month vacation in the summer. The school day in France is from 8 a.m. to 4 p.m. with a two-hour lunch **break**. Students

3   Samuel is from Kenya. He says, "Our **academic** year starts in June. The year has three terms, and each term lasts for 13 weeks. That feels like a long time. We get a one-month break after each term. The school day in Kenya begins at 8 a.m. and ends at 4 p.m. Students pay for school. It's not free like in some other countries.

We wear **uniforms** to school each day. All the uniforms are the same color, so they're really boring. We study many subjects, but I think the best part of school is soccer in the afternoon."

USA

4   Linda lives in the United States. She says, "School begins in late August and ends in June. Then we have a nine-week summer vacation. We attend school about 180 days each year. The school day is about seven hours long. I have six classes and one **study period**. I like math best. Every night, I do homework for about four hours. I don't have time to relax because my schedule is very busy!"

5   Marie, Samuel, and Linda all think they spend too much time in school. But the amount of time they spend in school is very different.

B. Read the statements. Write *T* (true) or *F* (false). Then correct each false statement to make it true.

__T__ **1.** Marie lives in France.

_____ **2.** There is a one-hour lunch break at school in France.

_____ **3.** In France, there are four terms in the school year.

_____ **4.** Students in France go to school from Monday to Saturday.

_____ **5.** The school year in Kenya begins in January.

_____ **6.** Kenyan schools are free.

_____ **7.** Students in Kenya wear uniforms.

_____ **8.** Students in the United States begin school in October.

_____ **9.** In the United States, there is a seven-week summer vacation.

C. Answer these questions.

1. How many weeks of school are there in France? _____

2. How many weeks of school are there in Kenya? _____

3. How many hours of class are there each day in Kenya? _____

4. How many hours of class are there each day in the United States? _____

5. Which country has the shortest school day? _____

D. Complete the sentences with information from the article.

1. Students in _____ don't have a long summer vacation.

   They have _____ one-month breaks during the year.

2. Students in France have a two-month _____ every summer.

3. In Kenya, students wear _____ to school.

4. Marie isn't happy about going to school on _____.

5. Linda takes _____ classes every day.

6. Linda spends _____ hours studying every night.

iQ ONLINE **E.** **Go online to read _Online High Schools_ and check your comprehension.**

Building Vocabulary | Word families

Word families are groups of similar words. Word families can include nouns, verbs, and adjectives. Learn words in word families, and learn the part of speech of each word.

Noun	Verb	Adjective
help	help	helpful
instructor	instruct	
student	study	studious

Do you need some **help**? (noun)
I can **help** you tomorrow. (verb)
My teacher is very **helpful**. (adjective)

Tip for Success

A vocabulary log is a list of new words. Use a vocabulary log to remember new words. Write each new word and a sentence with the word. You can make your log in a notebook, on note cards, or on your computer or tablet.

A. Label the underlined words. Write _N_ (noun), _V_ (verb), and _Adj_ (adjective).

1. Our school principal is a kind person. He is very <u>friendly</u> with the <u>students</u>.   _Adj_

2. My cousin <u>helps</u> me with my homework. He's <u>helpful</u>.

3. My brother is very <u>studious</u>. He <u>studies</u> about four hours every night.

4. I <u>study</u> at a math <u>academy</u> on Saturdays. I <u>enjoy</u> the classes there.

5. Our <u>academic</u> year starts in September.

6. For me, the most <u>enjoyable</u> part of the day is lunch.

Critical Thinking (Tip)

In Activity B, you **classify** words by the part of speech. Classifying information helps you see patterns so you can understand information better. For example, nouns often end in –*ty*: *difficulty, personality, university, popularity, activity.*

B. Complete the chart with words from Activity A. (An *X* means that the word doesn't exist or that you don't need to know it.)

	Noun	Verb	Adjective
1.	academy	X	*academic*
2.	difficulty	X	
3.	X		enjoyable
4.	friend	X	*friendly*
5.	help		
6.	intelligence	X	
7.		study	

iQ ONLINE **C. Go online for more practice with word families.**

Reading Skill | Scanning for names, dates, and times

You **scan** a text to find information quickly. When you scan, move your eyes quickly over the passage. Only look for the information you need.

Use these techniques to scan a reading.

1. To find information about a person, place, or country, look for capital letters.

☐ **Brian, New York, Egypt**

2. To find information about a day or month, look for capital letters.

☐ **Monday, October**

3. To find information about dates and times, look for numbers and abbreviations.

☐ in **2009**, at **8:30 a.m., five hours**

A. Scan the two paragraphs. Complete these steps.

1. Underline the names of the countries.

2. Circle the number of days in the school year.

3. Put two lines under the times of day and months of the year.

Schools in Germany

1   Jens lives in Germany. He says, "We start school at 7:30 in the morning. That's too early for me! Classes end at 1:30 p.m., so our school day is only six hours. Our school day is pretty short, but our school year is really long. The term begins in September and lasts until July. We take a short vacation in the summer—about six weeks. We study for 200 days each year. But I enjoy school. I study with my good friends, and we learn a lot of interesting things. I think our time in school is about right."

students in Germany

Schools Around the World

2   Around the world, students spend different numbers of days in school. For example, students in France study for 170 days each year, but in Australia, the school year is 200 days long. The number of hours each day is also different from country to country. The school day in France and Kenya is eight hours long and lasts from 8 a.m. to 4 p.m. But students in France get a two-hour break for lunch, so they only study for six hours a day. Students in Spain start school at 8:00 a.m. and attend class until 3:00 p.m. Their school day is seven hours long. In Germany, the school day is only six hours long.

students in Kenya

B. Answer these questions.

1. How long is the school year in France? _____

2. How long is the school day in Germany? _____

3. Which country has the shortest school year? _____

4. Which countries begin school at 8:00 a.m.? _____

5. Which country has school for seven hours a day? _____

C. Go online for more practice with scanning for names, dates, and times.

WRITE WHAT YOU THINK

A. Discuss these questions with a partner or in a group.

1. When do students at your school have vacation?

2. What time does school start and end every day?

3. What do students usually do during lunch?

4. Do students have a lot of homework?

B. Choose two questions from Activity A and write the answers. Look back at your Quick Write on page 23. Think about what you learned.

Question: _____

My answer: _____

_____

_____

_____

Question: _____

My answer: _____

_____

_____

_____

WRITING

UNIT OBJECTIVE ▶▶▶ At the end of this unit, you are going to write about a school. Your sentences will include information from the reading, the unit video, and your own ideas.

Writing Skill | Capitalization and punctuation

When you write, check for correct capitalization and punctuation.

Capitalization Rules

1. Capitalize the first word in a statement or question.

   I have a short study period every afternoon.
   Do young students usually wear uniforms?

2. Capitalize proper nouns: the names of people, places, languages, or things.

   My name is **Tim**. I'm from **San Diego**. I attend **City College**. I speak **English**.

3. Capitalize the days of the week and the months of the year.

   Classes start on **Monday, October** 12.

4. Capitalize *I*, even if it does not begin a sentence.

   My friend and **I** went to class.

Punctuation Rules

1. End every statement with a period (.).

   The high school has difficult academic classes.

2. End every question with a question mark (?).

   How much vacation time do you have every year?

A. Correct the mistakes in capitalization and punctuation.

1. are there many students in your classes

2. my exam is on february 3

3. the team practices every saturday for three hours

4. my classmate is from italy

5. our new teacher is from cairo, egypt

6. when is your lunch break

7. do you study in the library or at home

8. my cousin attends hong kong university

9. nour and majda both speak arabic

10. i work at super burger, and i wear a uniform

 B. Go online for more practice with capitalization and punctuation.

Grammar | Simple present

The simple present describes habits, facts, or feelings.

 **Tip for Success**

Remember to use the base verb + -s or -es after *he*, *she*, and *it*.

Affirmative statements

subject	verb	
I / You / We / They	**attend**	school on Saturday.
He / She	**attends**	

Negative statements

subject	*do/does* + *not*	verb	
I / You / We / They	**do not** **don't**	**take**	a lunch break.
He / She	**does not** **doesn't**		

Yes/No questions

do/does	subject	verb	
Do	you	**study**	hard?
Does	she	**have**	many friends?

Short answers

yes	no
Yes, I **do**.	No, I **don't**.
Yes, she **does**.	No, she **doesn't**.

Information questions

wh- word	*do/does*	subject	verb	
What	**do**	you	**talk**	about?
Where	**does**	he	**live?**	
When	**does**	she	**call**	you?

Answers

We **talk** about school.
He **lives** in Oman.
She **calls** me after dinner.

A. Complete each sentence to make it true for you. Use the correct form of the verb in parentheses. Use the negative (*don't / doesn't*) if necessary.

1. I _____*don't go*_____ to school Monday through Friday. (go)

2. At my school, students _____ uniforms. (wear)

3. I _____ a one-hour lunch break. (have)

4. A typical class _____ about 50 minutes. (last)

5. My best friend _____ my school. (attend)

6. I _____ sports after school. (play)

7. My English teacher _____ us a test every Friday. (give)

B. Write questions with *Do* or *Does*. Answer the questions. Then ask and answer the questions with a partner.

1. you and your friends / study together

   Do you and your friends study together? No, we don't.

2. your teacher / talk to you about college

   _____

3. your best friend / speak English well

   _____

4. you / like academic courses

   _____

5. your school / have a vacation soon

   _____

6. you / enjoy math classes

   _____

7. your teacher / give a lot of homework

   _____

C. Read about Rika. There are six mistakes. Correct the mistakes. The first one is done for you.

have
Do you ~~has~~ a busy academic life?

I do. My life at school is very busy. My school start at 7:00 every day. Classes last until 2:30 p.m. We not have a long lunch break. We have just 30 minutes, so we don't have much time to relax. We eat lunch in the cafeteria. I enjoy my classes, but they are difficult. My teachers are very helpful. My science teacher often help me after class. In the afternoon, I play soccer. Our school have an excellent soccer team. That is the best part of my day. At night I does homework.

Rika

D. Write questions. Then answer the questions.

1. When / Rika's school / start?

   <u>When does Rika's school start?</u>

   <u>It starts at 7:00.</u>

2. Where / Rika / eat lunch?

   _____

   _____

3. When / Rika's science teacher / help her?

   _____

   _____

 E. Go online for more practice with the simple present.

F. Go online for the grammar expansion.

In this assignment, you are going to write about a school. Think about the Unit Question, "Do students spend too much time in school?" Use the reading, the unit video, and your work in this unit. Look at the Self-Assessment checklist on page 34.

 Go to the Online Writing Tutor for a writing model and alternate Unit Assignments.

A. **BRAINSTORM** What words do we use to talk about schools? Write them in the chart. Then share your ideas with a partner.

Schedule/Time	Classes	Homework
busy	large	difficult

 B. **WRITE** Answer the questions about the school. Write complete sentences. Use your **BRAINSTORM** chart to help you. Go to *iQ Online* to use the Online Writing Tutor.

Writing **Tip**

Check your prepositions.
- Use *for* + amount of time (**for** 6 hours).
- Use *at* + specific time (**at** 3:00).
- Use *on* + day of the week (**on** Monday).
- Use *in* + month (**in** July).
- Use *from…to* with two times (**from** 8:00 **to** 3:00; **from** January **to** June).

1. What kind of school are you writing about?

2. When is the academic year?

3. How long is the summer vacation?

4. How long is the school day?

5. What do you like about the school?

6. What do you dislike about going to school?

7. How much time do students spend on homework each night?

8. Do you think students spend too much time in school?

C. REVISE Review your sentences with a partner. Read your partner's sentences. Then go online and use the Peer Review worksheet. Discuss the review with your partner.

D. EDIT AND REWRITE Complete the Self-Assessment checklist. Make final changes to your sentences. Be prepared to hand in your work or discuss it in class.

Yes	No	SELF-ASSESSMENT
☐	☐	Does every sentence start with a capital letter?
☐	☐	Does every sentence have a subject and a verb?
☐	☐	Are months and days of the week capitalized?
☐	☐	Does every sentence end with a period?
☐	☐	Check your verbs. Do you use the correct form of the simple present?
☐	☐	Do you use vocabulary from this unit?

E. REFLECT Go to the Online Discussion Board to discuss these questions.

1. What is something new you learned in this unit?

2. Look back at the Unit Question—Do students spend too much time in school? Is your answer different now than when you started the unit? If yes, how is it different?

TRACK YOUR SUCCESS

Circle the words you have learned in this unit.

Nouns	Verbs	Adjectives
academy AWL	attend	academic 🔑 AWL
break 🔑	enjoy 🔑	difficult 🔑
difficulty 🔑	last 🔑	enjoyable 🔑
help 🔑		studious
intelligence AWL		
study period		
term		
uniform 🔑 AWL		
vacation 🔑		

🔑 Oxford 2000 keywords

AWL Academic Word List

Check (✓) the skills you learned. If you need more work on a skill, refer to the page(s) in parentheses.

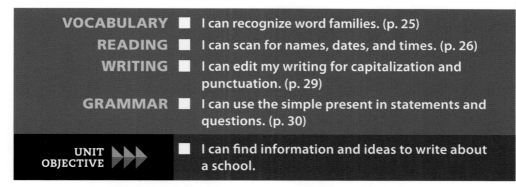

VOCABULARY	■ I can recognize word families. (p. 25)
READING	■ I can scan for names, dates, and times. (p. 26)
WRITING	■ I can edit my writing for capitalization and punctuation. (p. 29)
GRAMMAR	■ I can use the simple present in statements and questions. (p. 30)
UNIT OBJECTIVE ▶▶▶	■ I can find information and ideas to write about a school.

READING ▶ review: scanning for information
VOCABULARY ▶ using the dictionary
GRAMMAR ▶ adjectives and adverbs
WRITING ▶ writing complete sentences

UNIT QUESTION

When do we eat special foods?

A Work with a partner. Why do you usually eat? Check (✓) the boxes. Then discuss your ideas with your classmates.

I eat because . . .

☐ I'm hungry.   ☐ it's fun to do with friends.

☐ it's time for a meal.   ☐ I like to be with my family.

UNIT
OBJECTIVE ▶▶▶ Read a chapter from a textbook. Find information
and ideas to describe the people, food, and activities
at a celebration.

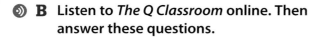

🔊 **B** **Listen to *The Q Classroom* online. Then
answer these questions.**

1. When do the students eat special foods?
   Match the name of the event to the student.

a. weekend	c. barbecue in the summer
b. holiday	d. celebrate something special

Event
Sophy	b. holiday
Yuna	
Marcus	
Felix	

2. Look at the photos. What special foods do you eat at celebrations?

iQ ONLINE **C** **Go to the Online Discussion Board to discuss the
Unit Question with your classmates.**

READING | Celebrating with Food

UNIT OBJECTIVE ▶▶▶

You are going to read a chapter from a textbook. The chapter is about celebrations of food around the world. Use the article to find information and ideas for your Unit Assignment.

PREVIEW THE READING

Vocabulary Skill Review

In Unit 2, you learned about word families. As you learn new vocabulary, remember to study other parts of speech in the same word family. In Activity A, how can you change the words *celebrate* and *prepare* to nouns?

A. **VOCABULARY** Here are some words from the reading. Look at the photos and read the sentences. Then write each <u>underlined</u> word next to the correct definition.

a. I use <u>ingredients</u> from my garden—tomatoes, peppers, and onions. I like <u>fresh</u> vegetables, not canned or frozen ones.

b. Weddings are a <u>special</u> time for people around the world. Most people <u>celebrate</u> their marriages by having a large party for their friends and family.

c. Cookouts are <u>popular</u> for summer holidays. Some <u>traditional</u> menus include grilled beef or chicken, potato salad, and fresh watermelon.

d. In Argentinian <u>culture</u>, Constitution Day is a holiday in May. Families <u>prepare</u> *pastelitos*, delicious fried cookies. They often enjoy them with a cup of hot tea.

1. _____ (*adjective*) not usual or ordinary

2. _____ (*adjective*) not frozen or in a can

3. _____ (*verb*) to make (a dish or a meal)

4. _____ (*verb*) to do something fun for a holiday

🔑 Oxford 2000 keywords

5. _____ (*adjective*) liked or enjoyed by a lot of people

6. _____ (*noun*) the things that you use to make a meal

7. _____ (*noun*) habits, ideas, or beliefs of a country

8. _____ (*adjective*) based on a belief or habit that started in the past and continues now

iQ ONLINE **B.** Go online for more practice with the vocabulary.

C. PREVIEW Look quickly over the chapter. Check (✓) the true statements.

☐ 1. The topic of this article is food in the United States.
☐ 2. There is a paragraph about a garlic festival.
☐ 3. There is a paragraph about a type of fish called herring.
☐ 4. The article describes food festivals in different countries.
☐ 5. The topic of this article is unusual vegetables.

garlic

D. QUICK WRITE Think about the food that you like to eat. Answer these questions with complete sentences. Use this section for your Unit Assignment.

1. What is your favorite food? _____

2. Who prepares the food? _____

3. When do you eat it? _____

herring

WORK WITH THE READING

A. Read the textbook chapter. Find information about special foods.

Celebrating with Food

1   People all around the world like to **celebrate** holidays, weddings, and the start of a new season with **special** food. Some **cultures** even celebrate food with special festivals! These festivals usually happen once a year. They can be fun and funny, but most of all, they're delicious.

2   One big food event, the Gilroy Garlic Festival, happens in July. The area around the town of Gilroy, California, produces huge amounts of garlic. Every year, over 4,000 volunteers provide food and entertainment for over 100,000 guests. Cooks **prepare** and sell many different types of dishes, all containing garlic. You can even buy garlic popcorn and garlic ice cream.

the Gilroy Garlic Festival

selling herring at the Baltic Herring Festival

3   The International White Truffle Fair happens in October in Alba, Italy. At the fair, visitors enjoy eating truffles, a kind of fungus. Truffles are a delicious **ingredient** in omelets, pasta, risotto, and rice. They can be very expensive; they sometimes cost $3,000 per pound (0.45 kilograms)!

5   Finally, a very popular festival happens in Gloucestershire, UK. This festival, called the Cooper's Hill Cheese-Rolling and Wake, is over 200 years old. Organizers of the event buy a large piece of cheese. It weighs over six pounds (2.72 kilograms). Then they drop it down a hill. As spectators watch and cheer, young men run down the hill after the cheese. There are ambulances at the bottom of the hill because people often fall and sometimes they get hurt. Cheese-rolling is dangerous, but it is a lot of fun.

white truffles

4   A very **traditional** food festival happens in Helsinki, Finland. The Baltic Herring Festival is over 270 years old and celebrates a **popular** fish, the herring. For one week in the month of October, fishermen sell fried herring, herring soup, herring sandwiches, and even herring pizza. You can buy **fresh** herring, too, and then take it home and make your own recipe. Other people sell handmade crafts and warm, wool clothes for the winter.

the Cooper's Hill Cheese-Rolling and Wake

B. Write the correct paragraph number next to each main idea.

a. There is a lot of garlic in Gilroy, California. ____

b. The cheese-rolling in Gloucestershire is a popular event. ____

c. People in some regions of the world like to celebrate the food they produce. ____

d. The Baltic Herring Festival is an old and traditional event. ____

e. You can find truffles in the Alba region of Italy. ____

C. Read the statements. Write _T_ (true) or _F_ (false). Then correct each false statement to make it true.

____ 1. Only people in Italy like to celebrate holidays with special food.

_____

____ 2. Special festivals with food usually happen once a month.

_____

____ 3. The Gilroy Garlic Festival has both food and entertainment.

_____

____ 4. You can get popcorn with garlic at the Gilroy Garlic Festival.

_____

____ 5. People eat a lot of chocolate at the International White Truffle Fair.

_____

____ 6. Truffles are not very expensive.

_____

____ 7. A herring festival is held each year in Oslo, Norway.

_____

____ 8. You can only buy fish at the herring festival.

_____

____ 9. People roll small pieces of cheese down Cooper's Hill.

_____

____ 10. People are sometimes hurt at the cheese rolling.

_____

D. Complete the sentences with information from the article.

1. People like to _____ holidays with special food.

2. Special festivals can be found in many different _____.

3. At the Gilroy Garlic Festival there is food and _____.

4. Cooks _____ and sell many kinds of food with garlic.

5. The International White Truffle Fair in Alba, Italy, takes place in the

   month of _____.

6. Truffles are an _____ in many different kinds of food.

7. The Baltic Herring Festival is more than _____ years old.

8. If you want to cook your own food, you can buy _____ herring.

9. At Cooper's Hill, people run down the hill after the _____.

10. People sometimes get hurt, so there are _____ at the bottom of the cheese-rolling hill.

Skill Review | Scanning for information

Remember: You scan a text to find information quickly. Only look for the information you need. To find information about a person, place, or country, look for capital letters. You can also scan for a specific word. Review the Reading Skill box in Unit 2, page 26.

E. **Read each question. Then scan the reading on pages 39–40 to find the underlined word. Answer the question.**

1. What product does the area around the town of <u>Gilroy</u> produce?

   _____

2. How much can one <u>pound</u> of truffles cost? _____

3. In what <u>month</u> is the Baltic Herring Festival? _____

4. Why are there <u>ambulances</u> at the Gloucestershire event? _____

   _____

5. "<u>Delicious</u>" is one way to describe food festivals. What are two other words used to describe them? _____

6. How many <u>volunteers</u> work at the Gilroy Garlic Festival? _____

iQ ONLINE **F.** **Go online to read *A Garden in the City* and check your comprehension.**

You can build your vocabulary by **using the dictionary**. Look at the entry.

> **fruit** 🔑 /frut/ **noun** [count, noncount]
>
> ❶ **PRONUNCIATION**
> The word **fruit** sounds like **boot**.
>
> the part of a plant or tree that holds the seeds. Oranges and apples are types of **fruit**: *Would you like **a piece of fruit**?* ◆ *"Would you like **some fruit**?" "Yes please – I'll have a pear."*

Use the dictionary entry to learn new words. In this definition for *fruit,* you can learn other important words: *plant*, *tree*, and *seeds*. You learn that oranges, apples, and pears are types of fruit. In addition, many learners' dictionaries have color illustrations to show vocabulary.

All dictionary entries are from the *Oxford Basic American Dictionary for learners of English* © Oxford University Press 2011.

Tip for Success

Learn words to describe food: *delicious, fresh, bitter, spicy, salty, sweet,* and *sour.* These adjectives answer the question, "How does it taste?"

A. Look at these dictionary entries. Answer the questions.

1.
> **meal** 🔑 /mil/ **noun** [count]
> food that you eat at a certain time of the day: *What's your favorite meal of the day?* ◆ *We **had** a nice **meal** in that restaurant.*
>
> **Culture**
>
> ■ **Breakfast**, **lunch**, and **dinner** are the usual meals of the day.
> ■ We do not usually use "a" with the names of meals: *Let's **have lunch** together tomorrow.*

a. What are three meals? _____

b. Write a sentence with the word *meal*. _____

_____

2.
> **veg·e·ta·ble** 🔑 /ˈvɛdʒtəbl/ **noun** [count]
> a plant or part of a plant that we eat: *The students grow vegetables such as cabbages, beans, and carrots.*

a. What are three other vegetables? _____

_____

b. Write a sentence with the word *vegetable*. _____

_____

B. Make a food chart. Add the words in the box, and then add more foods. If necessary, use a dictionary. Compare your chart with your partner.

apple	chicken	beef	lobster	milk	beans
onion	potato	shrimp	cheese	grapes	bananas

Fruit	Vegetables	Meat	Seafood	Dairy products
apple				

 **C.** Go online for more practice with using the dictionary.

 # WRITE WHAT YOU THINK

A. Ask and answer these questions with a partner. Look back at your Quick Write on page 39. Think about what you learned.

1. What is your favorite celebration?

2. When do you usually have this celebration?

3. What special foods do you eat? Why?

4. What is your favorite food at this celebration?

 B. Go online to watch the video about Japanese bento boxes. Then check your comprehension.

> **edible** *(adj.)* good or safe to eat
> **flavor** *(n.)* the taste of food
> **fried** *(adj.)* cooked in hot fat or oil
> **steamed** *(adj.)* cooked in steam (the gas that water becomes when it gets very hot)

VIDEO VOCABULARY

C. Think about the unit video and the reading as you discuss these questions. Then choose one question and write 3–5 sentences.

1. What kind of food is very special for you?

2. How would you describe your favorite celebration?

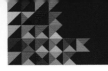

WRITING

▶▶▶ At the end of this unit, you are going to write about the people, food, and activities at a celebration. Your sentences will include information from the reading, the unit video, and your own ideas.

Grammar   Adjectives and adverbs

Adjectives

1. Adjectives describe nouns (people, places, or things).

   An adjective can come after the verb *be*. It describes the subject.

subject (noun)	*be*	adjective
Ice cream	is	**cold.**
The sandwiches	are	**huge.**

   An adjective can come before a noun. It describes the noun.

	adjective	noun
This is a	**traditional**	wedding.
I'm celebrating a	**special**	day.

2. There are no singular or plural adjectives.

   ✓ Correct: **popular**
   ✗ Incorrect: populars

3. Do not use an article (*the*, *a*, or *an*) before an adjective with no noun.

   ✓ Correct: This is a **delicious** meal. This is **delicious**.
   ✗ Incorrect: This is a delicious.

Adverbs + adjectives

Adverbs can be used to describe adjectives.

pizza

The pizza is **very hot.**
The vegetables are **really fresh.**
The food is **very good.**

Our dinner is **quite expensive.**
She is **extremely hungry.**
It's a **very popular** festival.

Learn adjectives in pairs of opposites. For example, *hot—cold* or *big—small*. Write them down.

A. (Circle) the adverb and <u>underline</u> the adjective in each sentence.

1. The garlic festival is (very) <u>popular</u>.

2. This is a really big pizza.

3. The cheese is quite expensive.

4. Leila's recipe is really good.

5. The tea is really hot!

6. These are extremely fresh vegetables.

7. Our town has a very special festival.

8. This is a very small sandwich.

9. That is an extremely big truffle.

10. They enjoy really delicious food.

B. There is one error in each sentence. Find the errors and correct them.

chicken noodle soup

1. It's a nice really garden.

2. This is a good dinner extremely.

3. Jim's vegetables are expensives.

4. The festival is quite a popular.

5. This food is bad extremely.

6. The chicken noodle soup is a delicious.

7. All of the ingredients are expensive quite.

8. The summer festivals are very bigs.

C. Go online for more practice with adjectives and adverbs.

D. Go online for the grammar expansion.

Writing Skill | **Writing complete sentences**

Every sentence needs a **subject** and a **verb**. The **subject** is a noun or pronoun. It answers the question, "Who or what is the sentence about?" The **verb** is the action. It answers the question, "What does the subject do, think, or feel?"

<u>I</u> <u>prepare</u> dinner every day.
subject verb

Usually <u>my dinners</u> <u>are</u> delicious.
              subject   verb

<u>My friends</u> <u>like</u> to go to cafés.
   subject   verb

Right now, <u>they</u> <u>are</u> at a café.
               subject verb

The **subject** can be **singular** or **plural**. *Singular* means "one." *Plural* means "more than one." The subject can be a noun or a pronoun.

	Singular	Plural
	bed	beds
	backpack	backpacks
	John	John and Mary
	I	we
	you (1 person)	you (more than one person)
	he, she, it	they

Always make your subject and verb agree.

✓ Correct: I like oranges.   ←   Subject and verb agree.

✓ Correct: He likes oranges.   ←   Subject and verb agree.

✗ Incorrect: He like oranges.   ←   Subject and verb do not agree.

A. Add a subject (*he*, *she*, *it*, or *they*) or the verb *be* to each sentence.

1. My brother ^is^ a student in a cooking program.

2. Is a very difficult book.

3. There delicious dishes on this menu.

4. Are very good cookies.

5. Is an excellent baker.

6. Kate at the café this afternoon.

7. I rarely eat seafood because it usually very expensive.

8. Hatem likes to eat in restaurants because doesn't like cooking.

B. Correct the incorrect verb in each sentence.

1. Sam ~~go~~ *goes* to the cafeteria after class.

2. Mary have a new job as a waitress.

3. They loves to eat ice cream in the park.

4. Hassan prepare coffee every morning.

5. I are at the same table as my friends.

6. Isabel don't like baking cakes.

7. We like eating chicken on Saturdays, and we usually has steak on Sundays.

C. Complete the paragraph. Use the correct verb forms.

At Chinese New Year we celebrate with traditional foods. First, we usually

_____ *eat* _____ round dumplings. These dumplings _____
    1. (eat)   2. (be)

small pieces of meat wrapped in a covering. Then we _____ to
                                                        3. (like)

eat duck. It _____ a lot like chicken. I _____ eating
              4. (taste)   5. (enjoy)

long noodles. We also _____ fish. The fish _____ a
                        6. (prepare)   7. (be)

wish for a happy year ahead. Sometimes people _____ a special
                                                  8. (eat)

vegetarian dish. This dish _____ only vegetables in it. After seven
                            9. (have)

days we enjoy a special salad. Everyone also _____ cake. The
                                                10. (eat)

cake _____ very popular.
      11. (be)

D. Write sentences about yourself with the words in parentheses. Change the verb if necessary. Label the subject and verb in each sentence.

                        S   V
1. (enjoy going out) _I enjoy going out for breakfast._____

2. (avoid eating) _____

3. (like to eat) _____

4. (enjoy preparing) _____

5. (like to celebrate) _____

E. Put the words in the correct order to make sentences.

1. They / delicious / prepare / pizzas

   _____

2. soup / The / is / hot / extremely

   _____

3. Mr. Adams / garden / grows / vegetables / large / very / in his

   _____

4. fresh / food / really / The / is

   _____

5. Everyone / festival / enjoys celebrating / the popular / at /

_____

6. like / ice cream / good / We

_____

7. The TV show / funny / very / is

_____

8. likes / hot / James / tea

_____

9. Lisa / special / prepares / food / for the holiday

_____

 **F.** Go online for more practice with writing complete sentences.

Unit Assignment   Describe the people, food, and activities at a celebration

 In this assignment, you are going to write about the people, food, and activities at a celebration. Think about the Unit Question, "When do we eat special foods?" Use the reading, the unit video, and your work in this unit. Look at the Self-Assessment checklist on page 50.

 Go to the Online Writing Tutor for a writing model and alternate Unit Assignments.

A. BRAINSTORM Look at the categories in the idea map below. Then draw an idea map. Complete the map with words about a special meal or celebration. Then explain your map to a partner.

When?   Where?   Why?

Special meal or celebration

People   Food   Activities

B. WRITE Answer the questions. Use complete sentences. Use your **BRAINSTORM** notes to help you. Go to *iQ Online* to use the Online Writing Tutor.

Writing Tip

Answer these questions when describing something: *Who? What? When? Where? Why? How?* This will add information to your description.

1. What is the special meal or celebration?

2. When does it happen?

3. What do you need to do before the meal?

4. Do you enjoy preparing the food? Why or why not?

5. Where do you have the meal?

6. Who comes to the celebration?

7. What are the main dishes?

8. Why is the food special?

9. Which food do you love eating?

10. Which food do you avoid eating? Why?

C. REVISE Review your sentences with a partner. Read your partner's sentences. Then go online and use the Peer Review worksheet. Discuss the review with your partner.

D. EDIT AND REWRITE Complete the Self-Assessment checklist. Make final changes to your sentences. Be prepared to hand in your work or discuss it in class.

SELF-ASSESSMENT		
Yes	No	
☐	☐	Does every sentence have a subject and a verb?
☐	☐	Do your subjects and verbs agree with each other?
☐	☐	Do you use adverbs and adjectives to add more information?
☐	☐	Do you use vocabulary from the unit?
☐	☐	Does every sentence start with a capital letter and end with a period?

E. REFLECT Go to the Online Discussion Board to discuss these questions.

1. What is something new you learned in this unit?

2. Look back at the Unit Question—When do we eat special foods? Is your answer different now than when you started the unit? If yes, how is it different?

TRACK YOUR SUCCESS

Circle the words you have learned in this unit.

Nouns	Verbs	Adjectives
ambulance	avoid 🔑	delicious
celebration	celebrate 🔑	expensive 🔑
culture 🔑 AWL	prepare 🔑	fresh 🔑
dairy		huge 🔑
festival 🔑		popular 🔑
fruit 🔑		special 🔑
ingredient		traditional AWL
meal 🔑		**Adverbs**
meat 🔑		extremely 🔑
product 🔑		quite 🔑
seafood		really 🔑
vegetable 🔑		
volunteer AWL		

🔑 Oxford 2000 keywords

AWL Academic Word List

Check (✓) the skills you learned. If you need more work on a skill, refer to the page(s) in parentheses.

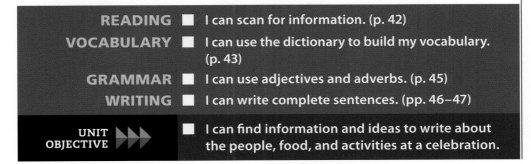

READING	☐ I can scan for information. (p. 42)
VOCABULARY	☐ I can use the dictionary to build my vocabulary. (p. 43)
GRAMMAR	☐ I can use adjectives and adverbs. (p. 45)
WRITING	☐ I can write complete sentences. (pp. 46–47)
UNIT OBJECTIVE ▶▶▶	☐ I can find information and ideas to write about the people, food, and activities at a celebration.

UNIT **4**

Sociology

VOCABULARY ▶ verb + noun collocations
READING ▶ underlining and highlighting
WRITING ▶ capitalizing proper nouns
GRAMMAR ▶ subject and object pronouns

Q

UNIT QUESTION

How do you have fun?

A Check (✓) the activities you enjoy. Put an *X* by activities you don't enjoy. Then compare with a partner.

☐ cooking
☐ playing sports
☐ going to the beach
☐ playing games

☐ watching TV
☐ telling jokes
☐ watching sports
☐ going out to eat

UNIT
OBJECTIVE ▶▶▶ Read some Web posts. Find information and ideas to
write about how you have fun with your friends.

B Listen to *The Q Classroom* online. Then answer these questions.

1. What did the students say?

2. Which student do you agree with? Why?

 C Go online to watch the video about board games. Then check your comprehension.

appreciate *(v.)* to enjoy something

board games *(n.)* games that you play on a board, for example chess

give up *(v.)* to stop trying to do something

tradition *(n.)* something that people in a particular place have done for a long time

 D Go to the Online Discussion Board to discuss the Unit Question with your classmates.

READING | No Money? Have Fun Anyway!

UNIT OBJECTIVE ▶▶▶ You are going to read Web posts about fun things to do without much money. Use the posts to find information and ideas for your Unit Assignment.

PREVIEW THE READING

A. **VOCABULARY** Here are some words from the reading. Read the definitions. Then complete each sentence.

> **events** *(noun)* 🔑 important things that happen
>
> **guess** *(verb)* 🔑 to give an answer when you do not know if it is right
>
> **invite** *(verb)* 🔑 to ask someone to come to a celebration, to your home, etc.
>
> **nature** *(noun)* 🔑 plants and animals
>
> **program** *(noun)* 🔑 a show on television or the radio
>
> **sightseeing** *(noun)* visiting interesting buildings and places as a tourist
>
> **support** *(verb)* 🔑 to help or encourage someone

🔑 Oxford 2000 keywords

Vocabulary Skill Review

In Unit 3, you learned to read examples in a dictionary entry. What example do you think the dictionary might give for the word *nature*?

1. My friends and I enjoy _____ when we travel to new cities.

2. I like to hike in the mountains because I enjoy _____.

3. Toshi wants to _____ us to come over for dinner.

4. I saw a famous person today. Can you _____ her name?

5. There is an interesting science _____ on TV tonight.

6. This newspaper lists the _____ of the weekend.

7. My school's soccer team has a big game tonight. I'll go and _____ them.

B. Work with a partner. Ask and answer these questions.

1. Do you support any sports teams? Which ones?

2. Do you like to spend time in nature? Where do you go?

3. Where do you like to go sightseeing?

4. What kind of events do you enjoy?

5. What is your favorite TV program? Why do you like it?

 C. Go online for more practice with the vocabulary.

D. PREVIEW These Web posts are about fun things to do without much money. Look quickly at the Web posts. Write three things the people like to do.

1. _____

2. _____

3. _____

E. QUICK WRITE Think about fun things to do in your area. Answer these questions. Use this section for your Unit Assignment.

1. If you have money, what is a fun weekend activity?

   _____

2. If you don't want to spend money, what is a fun activity?

   _____

WORK WITH THE READING

A. Read the Web posts. Find information about how to have fun without much money.

No Money? Have Fun Anyway!

James, New York Posted: 3 days ago	**Question:** How do you have fun without much money? Hi, everyone. I want to have fun, but I don't have much money. I need ideas. What can you do for free?
Anna, Miami Posted: 3 days ago	**1. Re:** How do you have fun without much money? James, why don't you go to your school's sporting **events**? I go to games every weekend. I watch soccer, basketball, baseball games, everything! It's fun to spend time with friends and **support** the school. And it's free!
Razi, Dubai Posted: 2 days ago	**2. Re:** How do you have fun without much money? I go window shopping with my friends! We go to expensive stores, but we only look—we don't buy anything. So it doesn't cost anything.
Isabel, Santiago Posted: 12 hours ago	**3. Re:** How do you have fun without much money? Our family likes going to the park. We take walks and enjoy **nature** there. Sometimes we have coffee and watch people. We try to **guess** their names and jobs. Try it!

Carlos, El Salvador Posted: 4 hours ago	**4. Re:** How do you have fun without much money? **Invite** some friends to your house and cook together! My friends and I cook together once a month. First, we decide on a meal. Then we shop for the ingredients and prepare the food. We usually cook food from a different country. My favorite was from Brazil. It's fun to eat with friends and try new recipes.
Khalid, Cairo Posted: 2 hours ago	**5. Re:** How do you have fun without much money? I like to just stay home and watch TV. There are lots of good **programs**, and it's free. That's the best way to have fun.
Rob, London Posted: 2 hours ago	**6. Re:** How do you have fun without much money? **Sightseeing** is fun, and you don't have to be a tourist. You can take a vacation in your own city. Walk around and enjoy the famous places.
James, New York Posted: 1 hour ago	**7. Re:** How do you have fun without much money? Thanks, everyone, for all of your ideas. I'll try some of them!

sightseeing

B. Match the person with the activity.

1. Anna ____
2. Razi ____
3. Isabel ____
4. Carlos ____
5. Khalid ____
6. Rob ____

a. go sightseeing
b. watch TV
c. go window shopping
d. cook with friends
e. watch people in the park
f. watch sports

Critical Thinking **Tip**

In Activity C, you **classify** information in a chart. Classifying information is a good way to organize your notes about a reading.

C. Complete the chart with information from the article. List the activities.

Fun activities at home	Fun activities away from home

D. Answer the questions. Use information from the reading on pages 56–57. Write complete sentences.

1. Why is it fun to watch school sporting events? _____

_____

2. What are three things to do in the park? _____

_____

3. Which activity costs some money? _____

_____

4. Where can you go sightseeing? What are two things to do? _____

_____

E. Circle the main idea for each of the posts in the reading.

1. Anna
   a. It's good to support your school.
   b. School sporting events are fun and free.
   c. You can watch your favorite sports at school events.

2. Razi
   a. Window shopping is fun, and you don't have to buy anything.
   b. Shopping with friends is fun.
   c. Window shopping at expensive stores is fun.

3. Isabel
   a. We like to go to the park and watch people there.
   b. We like to enjoy nature, and it is free.
   c. We like people watching.

4. Carlos
   a. Invite some friends to your house.
   b. Try different foods from different countries.
   c. Plan and cook a meal together with friends.

5. Khalid
   a. I like to watch TV at home.
   b. I like to stay home.
   c. Programs and movies on TV are free.

6. Rob
   a. Take a vacation and relax at home.
   b. Go sightseeing in another city.
   c. Go sightseeing in your own city.

 F. Go online to read *Walking in Barcelona* and check your comprehension.

Building Vocabulary | Verb + noun collocations

Collocations are words that we often use together. For example, we use the verb *play* with the noun *soccer*.

☐ I **play soccer.**

We don't use the verbs *do* or *go* with *soccer*.

☐ ✗ Incorrect: I do soccer.
☐ ✗ Incorrect: I go soccer.

Other collocations:

☐ give someone a ride   have an idea
☐ take a trip   make friends

give someone a ride

A. In each collocation, circle the verb. Underline the noun.

1. Lisa and Nora **are having coffee** together.

2. Let's **make plans** for Saturday night.

3. I **have an idea**! Let's go to the zoo.

4. Toshi **has fun** learning Spanish.

5. Mary **takes a walk** every day.

6. He **makes friends** with new people easily.

7. Are you hungry? **Have a snack**.

8. I am tired. I **am taking a vacation**!

9. **Tell** me **a joke**. I need to hear something funny.

10. Can you **give** me **a ride** to the mall?

B. Write a sentence using each collocation.

1. (to make plans) _____

2. (to have an idea) _____

3. (to have fun) _____

4. (to take a walk) _____

5. (to have coffee) _____

6. (to make friends) _____

7. (to have a snack) _____

8. (to take a vacation) _____

9. (to tell someone a joke) _____

Reading Skill	Underlining and highlighting

highlighting

When you read a text, <u>underline</u> or highlight the important information. This helps you remember it. Do not mark every word on the page. Mark *only* the important information.

Highlight or underline:

- The main idea or topic of a paragraph
- Information such as names, dates, or times

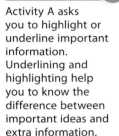

Critical Thinking **Tip**

Activity A asks you to highlight or underline important information. Underlining and highlighting help you to know the difference between important ideas and extra information.

A. Read the newspaper article. Highlight or underline the important information. Then answer the questions.

COMING EVENTS

1   **Storytelling.** Come listen to Jim Maddox and Mary Weston tell stories for a winter night on Wednesday, December 21, at 7 p.m. at the Davidson Library. Jim and Mary are well-known storytellers. Their stories are all about fun in the winter. Jim and Mary will also show their many photos of birds and animals. Come and enjoy a wonderful evening.

2   **Video contest.** High school students: Do you want to learn to make videos? We can teach you. The best video will win a prize of $250. We will also show the best three videos on our local TV station. For more information, meet at Town Hall at 2 p.m. on Thursday, December 22. You can borrow a camera from the library. Come learn, and improve your videos!

1. What is the date of the storytelling event? _____

2. Where will the storytelling event take place? _____

3. How much money is the prize in the video contest? _____

4. What time is the meeting for the video contest? _____

5. Where can you borrow a camera? _____

B. Look at the reading on pages 56–57 again. What fun activity does each person like? Underline or highlight the activity.

 C. Go online for more practice with underlining and highlighting.

 WRITE WHAT YOU THINK

A. Discuss these questions with a partner or in a group.

1. What activities are fun for shy and quiet people?

2. What activities are fun for outgoing and talkative people?

3. What activities are fun for serious people?

B. Choose two questions from Activity A and write answers. Look back at your Quick Write on page 55. Think about what you learned.

WRITING

UNIT OBJECTIVE

At the end of this unit, you are going to write about how you have fun with your friends. Your sentences will include information from the reading, the unit video, and your own ideas.

Writing Skill | Capitalizing proper nouns

A **noun** is a person, place, or thing. Nouns can be **proper nouns** or **common nouns**.

A proper noun is the name of a person, place, or thing. Proper nouns are always capitalized. This means some or all of the words begin with capital letters.

A common noun is a word for any person, place, or thing. Common nouns are usually only capitalized at the beginning of a sentence.

Proper Nouns		**Common Nouns**	
Maria Perez	New Zealand	woman	country
Tokyo	Spanish	city	nationality

Note: Many proper nouns have more than one word. Small words such as *the* and *of* are not usually capitalized in proper nouns.

the Red Sea   the Gulf of Aqaba

A. Read paragraph 1 of activity A on page 61. Circle the nine proper nouns.

B. Read each pair of nouns. Which is the common noun? Which is the proper noun? Write each proper noun with a capital letter.

1. boy   william   _____William_____

2. smith   last name   _____

3. subaru   car company   _____

4. friday   day of the week   _____

5. hard rock café restaurant   _____

6. november   month   _____

7. paris   place   _____

8. teacher   ms. andrews   _____

9. mountain   mount everest   _____

C. Go online for more practice with capitalizing proper nouns.

1. Subjects and objects can be nouns.
   - Subjects come before verbs in statements.
   - Objects come after verbs or prepositions, such as *at*, *in*, and *on*.

subject	verb	object	preposition + object
Kate	likes	the **book.**	
My **brother**	runs	—	in the **park.**

2. Pronouns replace nouns.
   - We use some pronouns for subjects.
   - We use some pronouns for objects.

	subject pronoun	object pronoun
singular	**I** enjoy playing video games.	Do you want to play with **me**?
	You are a good cook.	Let me give **you** a new recipe.
	He likes making videos.	Let's give **him** a new video camera.
	She is a very nice person.	I like **her** a lot.
	Where's the ball? **It**'s in the car.	Throw **it** to me!
plural	**We** like going to the beach.	Our friends always go with **us**.
	You always support our team.	We want to give **you** this team photo.
	They play soccer with us.	We always beat **them**.

3. We usually use pronouns *he/him*, *she/her*, *it/it*, *we/us*, and *they/them* after we've introduced the noun.

   Kate likes the book. **She** thinks **it**'s very interesting. (Kate = **she**; the book = **it**)

4. A **gerund** (verb + *-ing*) acts like a noun. The pronoun *it* replaces a gerund.

   I like **swimming**. **It**'s fun.

   gerund

A. Underline the pronouns. Then circle the noun that each pronoun refers to. Draw an arrow from the pronoun to the noun.

1. (Sarah and Jill) went to the mall. Then <u>they</u> went to a restaurant.

2. Matt likes to play tennis. He enjoys soccer, too.

3. Mika buys many books, but she doesn't always read them.

4. Ziyad will kick the ball, and Tomas will kick it back.

5. Hiro and Khalid like playing golf. They are pretty good, too!

6. Mary gave Emma and Tom some videos, and they gave her some books.

B. Complete each sentence with the correct subject or object pronoun.

1. <u>Tom</u> and I play tennis together. _____ usually wins.

2. <u>Anna</u> likes to play board games. _____ plays every weekend.

3. I don't like to play <u>golf</u>. I really hate _____.

4. <u>Mark</u> made a video, and I helped _____.

5. <u>Carlos and Isabel</u> came to my house. _____ cooked dinner.

6. <u>John and I</u> are going to take a walk. Maybe you can join _____.

 **C.** Go online for more practice with subject and object pronouns.

D. Go online for the grammar expansion.

Unit Assignment Write about how you have fun

 In this assignment, you are going to write about how you have fun with your friends. Think about the Unit Question, "How do you have fun?" Use the reading, the unit video, and your work in this unit. Look at the Self-Assessment checklist on page 66.

 Go to the Online Writing Tutor for a writing model and alternate Unit Assignments.

A. BRAINSTORM Answer the questions in the chart. Make notes, but don't write sentences. Then share your ideas with a partner.

Tip for Success

Make your writing more interesting by answering *Wh-* questions—*Who? What? When? Where? Why?*

What do you do for fun?	Why is this fun for you?	When do you do this?
1.		
2.		
3.		

B. WRITE Answer the questions. Write complete sentences. Use your **BRAINSTORM** notes to help you. Go to *iQ Online* to use the Online Writing Tutor.

1. What do you do for fun?
2. Where do you do this?
3. When do you do this?
4. Who do you do this with?
5. Why is this fun for you?

C. REVISE Review your sentences with a partner. Read your partner's sentences. Then go online and use the Peer Review worksheet. Discuss the review with your partner.

D. EDIT AND REWRITE Complete the Self-Assessment checklist. Make final changes to your sentences. Be prepared to hand in your work or discuss it in class.

SELF-ASSESSMENT		
Yes	No	
☐	☐	Do you use verb + noun collocations correctly?
☐	☐	Do you use subject and object pronouns correctly?
☐	☐	Do you capitalize proper nouns?
☐	☐	Does every sentence include a subject and a verb?
☐	☐	Do you use vocabulary from the unit?
☐	☐	Does every sentence start with a capital letter and end with a period?

E. **REFLECT** Go to the Online Discussion Board to discuss these questions.

1. What is something new you learned in this unit?

2. Look back at the Unit Question—How do you have fun? Is your answer different now than when you started the unit? If yes, how is it different?

TRACK YOUR SUCCESS

Circle the words and phrases you have learned in this unit.

Nouns	**Collocations**	make friends
event 🔑	give (someone) a ride	make plans
nature 🔑	go window shopping	play soccer
program 🔑	have a snack	take a trip
sightseeing	have an idea	take a vacation
Verbs	have coffee	take a walk
guess 🔑	have fun	tell a joke
invite 🔑		
support 🔑		

🔑 Oxford 2000 keywords

Check (✓) the skills you learned. If you need more work on a skill, refer to the page(s) in parentheses.

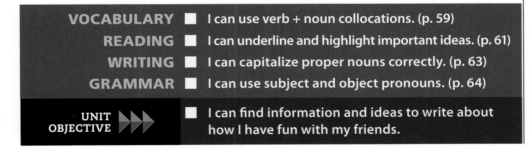

VOCABULARY	■	I can use verb + noun collocations. (p. 59)
READING	■	I can underline and highlight important ideas. (p. 61)
WRITING	■	I can capitalize proper nouns correctly. (p. 63)
GRAMMAR	■	I can use subject and object pronouns. (p. 64)
UNIT OBJECTIVE ▶▶▶	■	I can find information and ideas to write about how I have fun with my friends.

UNIT **5**

Architecture

READING ▶ review: underlining and highlighting
VOCABULARY ▶ word categories
GRAMMAR ▶ prepositions of location
WRITING ▶ subject-verb agreement in different
sentence types

UNIT QUESTION

What is your favorite room?

A Answer these questions. Then share your answers with a partner.

1. Describe your living room. What color is it? What is in it?

2. What do you like about your home? Where do you spend the most time?

3. Look at the photo. What do you see in this room? What do you like about this room? What do you dislike about this room?

B Listen to *The Q Classroom* online. Then answer these questions.

1. What does each person—Yuna, Felix, Marcus, and Sophy—say about their favorite rooms?

2. What reason does Sophy give for her answer?

3. Can you explain why you like your favorite room?

 C Go to the Online Discussion Board to discuss the Unit Question with your classmates.

READING 1 | There's No Place Like Home

UNIT OBJECTIVE ▶▶▶ You are going to read a Web page about people's favorite rooms. Use the Web page to find information and ideas for your Unit Assignment.

PREVIEW THE READING

A. **VOCABULARY** Here are some words from Reading 1. Read the sentences. Circle the correct explanation for the <u>underlined</u> words.

I think something is burning.

1. Jane: I think something is burning.
   Mark: Really? I have a bad cold. I can't <u>smell</u> anything.
   a. You smell something with your nose.
   b. You smell something with your eyes.

2. This chair is very <u>comfortable</u>. You can sit here and relax.
   a. The chair is expensive.
   b. The chair is nice to sit on.

3. My sisters always come into my bedroom without knocking. I have no <u>privacy</u>!
   a. I have no space or time away from others.
   b. I have no time to do my homework.

4. I <u>share</u> a bedroom with my two brothers.
   a. My brothers and I have our own bedrooms.
   b. My brothers and I have the same bedroom.

5. John is a very <u>calm</u> person. He never worries or gets angry.
   a. John is a very relaxed person.
   b. John fights with a lot of people.

6. Mary <u>collects</u> postcards. She has 300 postcards from around the world.
   a. She saves postcards as a hobby.
   b. She sells postcards for a job.

7. There are four windows in the kitchen. The room is very <u>bright</u>.
   a. The kitchen is very dark.
   b. The kitchen is full of light.

Vocabulary Skill Review

As you learn new vocabulary, remember that collocations are words that we often use together. For example, the verb *share* is often followed by the nouns *stories, ideas,* or *thoughts*. The verb *collect* is often followed by the noun *information* or things like *posters, books, stamps,* etc.

🔑 Oxford 2000 keywords

8. Hassan <u>spends time</u> with his grandparents on Sundays. Usually they have dinner together.

    a. Hassan doesn't have time to see his grandparents on Sundays.

    b. On Sundays, Hassan visits his grandparents for a few hours.

B. Answer these questions.

1. Who do you like to spend time with? _____

2. Where do you go to feel calm? _____

3. Where do you go to have privacy? _____

4. What is something that you share with others? _____

5. Do you collect anything? What? _____

 C. Go online for more practice with the vocabulary.

D. PREVIEW Quickly scan the Web page to answer these questions.

1. What rooms do people describe? _____

    _____

2. What countries are the people from? _____

    _____

E. QUICK WRITE Think about a room in your house. Answer these questions. Use this section for your Unit Assignment.

1. What color is the room? _____

2. What are some things in the room? _____

    _____

3. What do you usually do in the room? _____

    _____

WORK WITH THE READING

A. Read the Web page to find information about people's favorite rooms.

There's No Place Like Home

Home and Life Magazine

Last week I asked readers about their favorite rooms in their homes. Wow! I got some great answers and photos! Enjoy reading! And remember, there's no place like home!

1   I love to cook, so my favorite room is the kitchen. It always **smells** delicious. There is a large window, and you can see the garden from it. Next to the window, there is a small round table. My family and I often have breakfast at that table, but we eat dinner in the dining room.

Makiko, Japan

2   My favorite room is the family room because I love being with my family. It's a **comfortable** room with a sofa, a TV, bookshelves, and cabinets. There are family photos on the bookshelf. To the left of the TV, there is a fireplace.

Jane, United States

3   My favorite room is my bedroom. I have a lot of **privacy** because I don't **share** my room with my younger brother. My bedroom is very small, and the colors are boring. My bed is black and my carpet is gray. But I feel **calm** in my room. I **collect** posters, so there are posters of cars, surfers, and animals on the walls.

Ethan, United States

4   My favorite room is the dining room. On the weekends, we relax and enjoy meals here with my sister and her husband. We sit around a big table. There are several big windows, so the room is **bright** and sunny.

Samira, Lebanon

5 I love to **spend time** in the basement. Why?
Because my friends and I have a lot of fun there!
We play games and relax. We can make a lot of
noise, too. There's a drum set, a TV with video
games, and board games. There's a big sofa, too.

Hans, Germany

B. Answer these questions.

1. What does Hans like to do?

   _____

2. Why does Makiko like the kitchen?

   _____

3. Who likes a room for privacy?

   _____

4. Who writes about spending time with family members?

   _____

5. Who writes about a place to spend time with friends?

   _____

C. Circle the correct words to complete these statements.

1. Makiko's family eats (breakfast / dinner) at the table in the kitchen.

2. There's a large (window / table) in Makiko's kitchen.

3. Jane's family room has a (large table / TV).

4. Jane's family room is very (comfortable / messy).

5. Ethan collects (posters / cards) of surfers.

6. It's sunny in Samira's (dining room / kitchen).

7. Hans likes to be (quiet / loud) in the basement.

8. There's a (sofa / bed) in Hans's basement.

D. Complete these sentences.

Makiko is from _____ . Her favorite room is the

_____ . She likes it because it always _____
      2   3

very good. She also enjoys looking out the _____ at the
                                                 4

_____ . Her family often eats _____ in the
     5   6

kitchen.

Jane likes to spend time with her _____ in the family
                                           7

room. She likes it because it is _____ . In the family room,
                                      8

they can watch _____ .
                            9

Ethan likes his _____ because he has a lot of
                          10

_____ there. His bedroom is _____ and the
     11   12

colors are _____ . But he feels _____ in his
                    13   14

room. On the walls you can see a lot of _____ .
                                     15

Samira is from _____ . Her family likes to
                         16

_____ and enjoy meals in their _____ room.
     17   18

The room is _____ and sunny.
                        19

Hans likes to spend time in the _____ . He and his
                                20

friends have a lot of _____ there. They like to play
                          21

_____ and _____ .
     22   23

E. Complete each sentences with a word or phrase from the box.

a big table	black	the garden	noise	The TV

1. Makiko can see _____ from her kitchen.

2. _____ is near the fireplace in Jane's house.

3. Ethan's bed is _____ .

4. Samira's family sits around _____ .

5. Hans and his friends make a lot of _____ .

WRITE WHAT YOU THINK

A. Discuss these questions with a partner or in a group.

1. Look at the pictures in Reading 1 on pages 72–73. Which room do you like best? Why?

2. Do you have all of these rooms in your home? Are there any that you don't have?

3. Which person would you like to visit? Why do you want to visit them?

B. Choose one or two questions from Activity A. Write your answers. Look back at your Quick Write on page 71. Think about what you learned.

READING 2 | A Tall Man in a Small Space

UNIT OBJECTIVE ▶▶▶▶ You are going to read a newspaper article about one man's very small apartment. Use the article to find information and ideas for your Unit Assignment.

PREVIEW THE READING

A. **VOCABULARY** Here are some words from Reading 2. Read the definitions. Then complete the sentences.

> **design** (verb) 🔑 to draw a plan
> **extra** (adjective) 🔑 more than usual
> **however** (adverb) 🔑 but
> **modern** (adjective) 🔑 new, up-to-date; not traditional
> **own** (verb) 🔑 to have something
> **space** (noun) 🔑 an open area
> **view** (noun) 🔑 things you can see

 Oxford 2000 keywords

1. My bedroom has a big closet. I have a lot of _____ for my clothes.

2. Sun-Hee has _____ furniture in her home. She doesn't like old styles and designs.

3. The soup doesn't look very good. _____, it smells delicious.

4. Rob likes to _____ cars. His drawings are fantastic.

5. We have a(n) _____ bedroom in our house. Our guests stay in it when they visit.

6. My bedroom window has a nice _____ of the street below. I like to watch people walk by.

7. I don't _____ an air conditioner. I plan to buy one soon.

iQ ONLINE **B.** **Go online for more practice with the vocabulary.**

C. **PREVIEW** **Scan the article for information. Complete these sentences.**

1. Steve Sauer spent _____ years building his apartment.

2. Under a large yellow square on the floor is a _____.

3. The most interesting parts of the apartment are the _____ and the TV area.

D. **QUICK WRITE** **What are some good reasons to live in a small apartment? Write a list. Use this section for your Unit Assignment.**

Skill Review Underlining and highlighting

Remember: You can underline or highlight important information as you read. Underline one or two important words or phrases in each paragraph. Review the Reading Skill box in Unit 4, page 61.

A. Read the article to find information about people's favorite rooms.

A Tall Man in a Small Space

1   Steve Sauer is a very tall man. He's 6 feet 2 inches (187 cm), but he lives in an extremely small apartment. It's only 11 feet by 16 feet (3.35 by 4.88 meters). **However**, this isn't a problem for Sauer. He loves his small apartment. Sauer doesn't like **extra**, unused **space**, and he doesn't **own** many things.

2   Sauer spent seven years building his tiny apartment. He **designed** it, and he also designed and built some of the furniture. The apartment has many open areas. It doesn't have many walls or doors. It has a kitchen with a dining area, a bathroom, two beds, a TV area, and a reading area. In addition, he has space for his two bicycles.

Sauer's kitchen and dining area

3   When you come in the front door, there is a hall. The bathroom is on the left. Next to the bathroom is the kitchen. In the hall near the kitchen counter, there is a large yellow square on the floor. Lift it up, and you see a beautiful bathtub under the floor.

4   The most interesting parts of the apartment are the beds and the TV area. There is one bed above the bathroom. The other bed is above the closet, at the end of the hall. The TV area is beside the closet. It's a small but relaxing place to watch TV. Above this area, across from the bed, there is a small reading area. It's next to a big window. There is a sunny **view** of the street.

5   Sauer loves his tiny apartment. It is **modern** and neat. There is a place for everything important, but there is no space for extra or unnecessary things. In his free time, he loves to design and build things for small spaces. What's his job? He's an interior designer[1] for airplanes!

Steve Sauer in his apartment

[1] **interior designer:** a person who designs the inside of a building or other indoor space

B. Write the correct paragraph number next to each main idea.

____ a.   The beds and the TV area are very interesting and unusual.

____ b.   Sauer likes to design things for small spaces.

____ c.   Sauer is a tall man, but he lives in a tiny apartment.

____ d.   In the hallway, there is a bathtub under the floor.

____ e.   Sauer designed and built his apartment and some of the furniture.

Tip for Success

Often you can understand something better when you see it. A diagram or a drawing can help you see (or visualize) what you read. This can improve your reading comprehension.

C. Work with a partner. Scan the article again and look at the photos. Label the areas in Sauer's apartment.

| bathroom | bed | ~~closet~~ | reading area |
| bathtub | bed | kitchen | TV area |

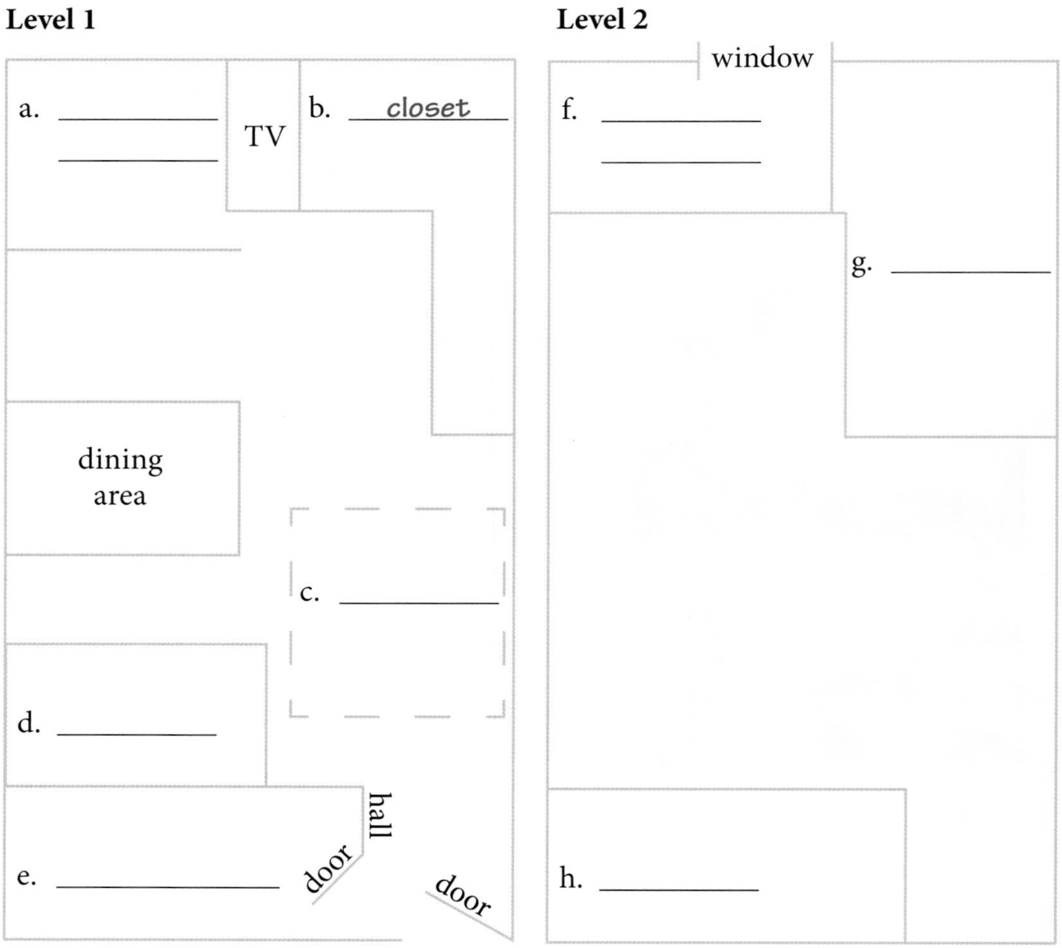

Level 1

a. _____ _____   TV

b. ___closet___

dining area

c. _____

d. _____

e. _____   door   hall   door

Level 2

window

f. _____ _____

g. _____

h. _____

D. Read the statements. Write *T* (true) or *F* (false). Then correct each false statement to make it true.

____ 1. The apartment is 10 feet by 16 feet (3.04 by 4.87 meters).

____ 2. Sauer worked on his apartment for seven years.

____ 3. The bathroom is on the right of the hall.

____ 4. There is a bathtub under the floor of the hall.

____ 5. The TV area is above the reading area.

____ 6. There is a big window in the reading area.

____ 7. The apartment is very modern.

____ 8. Sauer is an airplane mechanic.

E. Match the items with their locations.

____ 1. the kitchen   a. next to a big window

____ 2. a large yellow square   b. at the end of the hall

____ 3. the bathtub   c. near the kitchen counter

____ 4. one bed   d. above the bathroom

____ 5. the closet   e. under the floor

____ 6. a small reading area   f. next to the bathroom

F. Write the words from the reading that best complete the sentences.

bathtub	beds	bicycles	designed	neat
reading	small	space	tall	watching TV

Steve Sauer is very _____. His apartment is very

_____. Sauer _____ the apartment himself.
      2   3

There is no unused _____. The _____ is under
              4   5

the floor. The apartment has two _____. There is a small area
                    6

for _____ and another small area for _____.
   7   8

There is even space for Sauer's two _____. Sauer is not a
                    9

messy person. His apartment is modern and _____.
                                10

 **G.** Go online to read *Unusual Homes Around the World* and check your comprehension.

 WRITE WHAT YOU THINK

A. Discuss these questions with a partner or in a group. Look back at your Quick Write on page 76. Think about what you learned.

1. Do you like Sauer's apartment? Why or why not?

2. You can add one room to Sauer's apartment. What room do you want to add? Why?

3. Do you know someone with a very small apartment? Describe the apartment.

 B. Go online to watch the video about a famous house called Fallingwater. Then check your comprehension.

> **VIDEO VOCABULARY**
>
> **architect** *(n.)* a person who designs and plans buildings
> **dramatic** *(adj.)* sudden, great, or exciting
> **fantastic** *(adj.)* very good; wonderful
> **waterfall** *(n.)* a place where water falls from a high place to a low place

C. Think about the unit video, Reading 1, and Reading 2 as you discuss these questions. Then choose one question and write an answer.

1. In your home, which room has privacy? Describe the room.

2. In your home, where do you spend time with family or friends? Describe the room.

Question: _____

My answer: _____

_____

_____

_____

_____

Building Vocabulary | Word categories

Critical Thinking **Tip**

When you **categorize** things, you put them into groups. You can categorize ideas or opinions, types of people, types of entertainment, and so on. Categorizing helps you see similarities between things.

A category is a group of things. You can build your vocabulary by learning words in a category. For example, the category "rooms in a house" includes *living room*, *dining room*, *kitchen*, *bathroom*, and *bedroom*.

A room in a house can also be a category. Put words for furniture and appliances under the name of each room.

living room	bedroom	kitchen
sofa lamp	bed	refrigerator

A. In your vocabulary log, make a chart like the one in the Building Vocabulary box. Then write these words under the correct room. Some words can go in more than one room.

armchair	coffeemaker	dresser	mirror	sofa
bed	coffee table	fan	oven	stove
blender	desk	lamp	refrigerator	table
bookshelf	dishwasher	microwave	rug	toaster

B. With a partner, add more words to your charts. Write them under the correct room.

Tip **for Success**

Here are some useful adjectives to describe rooms:
large – small
sunny – dark
colorful – plain
modern – traditional

C. Ask and answer these questions with a partner.

1. What furniture is in your living room? What adjectives describe your living room?

2. What appliances are in your kitchen? What adjectives describe your kitchen?

3. What furniture is in your bedroom? What adjectives describe your bedroom?

D. Go online for more practice with word categories.

UNIT OBJECTIVE ▶▶▶▶ At the end of this unit, you are going to write about your favorite room. Your sentences will include information from the readings, the unit video, and your own ideas.

Grammar	Prepositions of location

Prepositions of location answer the question "Where?"

The student is sitting **at** his desk.

The ruler is **in** the desk drawer.

The light is **over** / **above** the desk.

The backpack is **under** the table.

The backpack is **on** the floor.

The trash can is **next to** / **beside** the desk.

The poster is **on** the wall.

The fan is **on the right of** the desk.

The bookshelf is **behind** the fan.

The fan is **in front of** the bookshelf.

A. Look at the picture. Write sentences with prepositions of location on page 83.

1. lamp / desk _The lamp is on the desk._____

2. poster / wall _____

3. bookshelf / bed _____

4. chair / desk _____

5. armchair / window _____

6. photos / bookshelf _____

B. **Read this paragraph about the picture in Activity A on page 82. There are five errors. Find them and correct them.**

I live in a very small apartment. It's crowded, but it's comfortable.
My desk is ~~beside~~ ^{under} my bed. In my desk, I have my computer and my
notebooks. To the left my desk, there is a small bookshelf. I have many
books at my bookshelf. There is an armchair over my desk. I like my
room, but next year I want more space for my clothes. I need a big closet.

C. **Look around your classroom. What do you see? Use the words to write sentences with prepositions of location.**

1. teacher's desk _The teacher's desk is next to the door._____

2. door _____

3. board _____

4. light _____

5. trash can _____

6. windows _____

7. computer _____

8. my desk _____

D. Go online for more practice with prepositions of location.

E. Go online for the grammar expansion.

In Unit 3, on page 46, you learned about subjects and verbs.

The **subject** and **verb** of a sentence must **agree** with each other. (A **singular** verb is used with a **singular** subject. A **plural** verb is used with a **plural** subject.)

subject verb
She **has** breakfast at the small round table.

subject verb
They **have** breakfast at the small round table.

subject verb
✗ The boys **shares** an apartment.
✓ The boys **share** an apartment.

If a sentence has more than one subject or verb, the verb(s) must still agree with the subject(s).

subject verb
My mother and father **collect** books.

subject verb
My brothers **put away** their clothes and **make** their beds.
verb

The subject and verb must agree in negative sentences.

subject verb
She **doesn't like** small rooms.

subject verb
Luis and Paul **don't like** the room.

subject verb
The room **isn't** very big.

subject verb
The rooms **aren't** very big.

The subject and verb must agree when used in **questions**.

verb subject
Are you at your apartment?

verb subject
Where **is** the bathroom?

verb subject verb
Does he **have** any posters in his room?

verb subject
Why **are** the closets small?

Tip for Success

Some verbs have
irregular forms:
*go–goes, do–does,
have–has, am–are–is*

A. Complete each sentence with a word from the box. You may need to change the verb to make it agree with the subject.

be	describe	eat	have	share
collect	design	do	like	smell

1. We _____ dinner at 6:30.

2. Can you _____ your room for me? What does it look like?

3. The architects _____ small apartments.

4. I _____ to spend time in the family room.

5. The kitchen always _____ delicious.

6. My desk _____ under the window.

7. Where _____ your family spend the most time?

8. That famous designer _____ his ideas with everyone.

9. William _____ coins from different countries.

10. Amanda and Kate _____ many books.

Tip for Success

Some nouns have
irregular plurals:
*man–men
woman–women
child–children
person–people
foot–feet
tooth–teeth*

B. Read the sentences. Write S if the subject is singular. Write P if the subject is plural. Then circle the correct verb form.

_P_ 1. Tamara and Mina (likes /(like)) to relax in the living room.

____ 2. The bedroom and reading area (provides / provide) privacy.

____ 3. Some people (enjoy / enjoys) meals in the kitchen.

____ 4. Ethan (likes / like) reading and relaxing at his house.

____ 5. Makiko's kitchen (has / have) a nice view of the garden.

____ 6. Jane's family room and living room (is / are) very comfortable.

____ 7. Steve (designs / design) and (builds / build) airplanes.

____ 8. Nabil (shares / share) his bedroom with his brother.

____ 9. The children (plays / play) computer games.

____ 10. Marie (doesn't like / don't like) small rooms.

C. Use *isn't/aren't* or *doesn't/don't* to make these sentences negative. Use a singular verb with a singular subject. Use a plural verb with a plural subject.

1. He enjoys the view. <u>He doesn't enjoy the view.</u>

2. The men are in the dining room. _____

3. The apartment is very comfortable. _____

4. The bathroom has a bathtub in it. _____

5. His friends play games in the basement. _____

6. I like to walk outside. _____

D. Write complete sentences. For each sentence, use one phrase from Group A and one phrase from Group B. Change the verb form if necessary. There are many different ways to combine the phrases.

Group A	Group B
My mother and father	have a nice apartment
The bedroom and the reading area	enjoy reading
Toshi	like animals
My brother	have a view of the garden
The people next door	be very noisy

1. <u>The people next door are very noisy.</u>

2. _____

3. _____

4. _____

5. _____

E. Make questions from the words. Change the verb form if necessary. Then answer the questions.

1. you / live / in a small apartment <u>Do you live in a small apartment?</u>

    <u>No, I live in a house with my family.</u>

2. the walls / in your bedroom / bright <u>Are the walls in your bedroom bright?</u>

    <u>Yes. They're bright yellow.</u>

3. your family / play games / together _____

_____

4. you / collect / posters _____

_____

5. your friends / spend lots of time reading _____

_____

6. your home / pretty comfortable _____

_____

 **F.** Go online for more practice with subject-verb agreement.

Unit Assignment Write about your favorite room

 In this assignment, you are going to write about your favorite room. Think about the Unit Question, "What is your favorite room?" Use the readings, the unit video, and your work in this unit. Look at the Self-Assessment checklist on page 88.

 Go to the Online Writing Tutor for a writing model and alternate Unit Assignments.

Writing Tip

You can use *there is* and *there are* to describe a room. The verb *be* agrees with the word after it: *There **is** a **closet**.* *There **are** some **shoes** on the floor.*

A. **BRAINSTORM** Draw a floor plan of your favorite room. Write words to describe it. Then describe your room to a partner.

My favorite room in my apartment is my living room. It's a large living room. There's a colorful sofa and two comfortable armchairs.

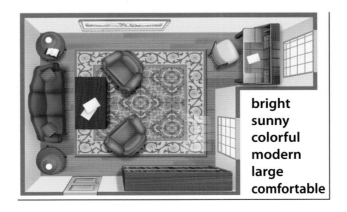

bright
sunny
colorful
modern
large
comfortable

B. **WRITE** Answer the questions. Use complete sentences. Use your **BRAINSTORM** floor plan and notes to help you. Go to *iQ Online* to use the Online Writing Tutor.

1. What is in the room? Where are these things?

2. What do you like to do in the room?

3. Why do you like it?

C. **REVISE** Review your sentences with a partner. Read your partner's sentences. Then go online and use the Peer Review worksheet. Discuss the review with your partner.

D. **EDIT AND REWRITE** Complete the Self-Assessment checklist. Make final changes to your sentences. Be prepared to hand in your work or discuss it in class.

SELF-ASSESSMENT		
Yes	**No**	
☐	☐	Do you use prepositions of location correctly?
☐	☐	Do you use correct subject-verb agreement?
☐	☐	Do you include vocabulary from the unit?
☐	☐	Do you use capitalization and punctuation correctly?

E. **REFLECT** Go to the Online Discussion Board to discuss these questions.

1. What is something new you learned in this unit?

2. Look back at the Unit Question—What is your favorite room? Is your answer different now than when you started the unit? If yes, how is it different?

TRACK YOUR SUCCESS

Circle the words and phrases you have learned in this unit.

Nouns
area 🔑 AWL
armchair
bookshelf
coffee table
coffeemaker
dishwasher
dresser
microwave
mirror 🔑
oven 🔑
privacy
refrigerator
sofa
space 🔑

stove 🔑
view 🔑

Verbs
collect 🔑
design 🔑 AWL
own 🔑
share 🔑
smell 🔑
spend time

Adjectives
bright 🔑
calm 🔑
comfortable 🔑
extra 🔑

modern 🔑
neat 🔑

Adverb
however 🔑

Prepositions
above 🔑
behind 🔑
beside 🔑
in front of 🔑
next to 🔑
on the right of
over 🔑
under 🔑

🔑 Oxford 2000 keywords
AWL Academic Word List

Check (✓) the skills you learned. If you need more work on a skill, refer to the page(s) in parentheses.

READING ☐	I can underline and highlight information. (p. 76)
VOCABULARY ☐	I can use categories to learn words. (p. 81)
GRAMMAR ☐	I can use prepositions of location. (p. 82)
WRITING ☐	I can use correct subject-verb agreement in different types of sentences. (p. 84)
UNIT OBJECTIVE  ☐	I can find information and ideas to write about my favorite room.

READING ▶ identifying pronoun references
VOCABULARY ▶ collocations
GRAMMAR ▶ modals *can*, *could*, and *should*
WRITING ▶ using an editing checklist

UNIT QUESTION

How can you change an unhealthy habit?

A Habits are regular activities. Look at the list of habits. Which habits are unhealthy? Check (✓) them. Then compare with a partner.

- ☐ sleep four hours every night
- ☐ eat fresh fruit every day
- ☐ drink a lot of coffee every day
- ☐ eat cookies and cake every day
- ☐ take a walk every morning
- ☐ drink a lot of water every day
- ☐ work all the time
- ☐ have sugary[1] drinks every day

B Listen to *The Q Classroom* online. Then answer these questions.

1. How does each person answer the question?

2. Can you think of other ways to change an unhealthy habit?

 C Go to the Online Discussion Board to discuss the Unit Question with your classmates.

[1] **sugary:** has a lot of sugar in it and tastes sweet

91

READING 1 | When Does a Change Become a Habit?

UNIT OBJECTIVE ▶▶▶▶ You are going to read a textbook excerpt about changing an unhealthy habit. Use the excerpt to find information and ideas for your Unit Assignment.

PREVIEW THE READING

A. VOCABULARY Here are some words from Reading 1. Read the definitions. Then complete the sentences below.

> **become** *(verb)* 🔑 to begin to be something
> **behavior** *(noun)* 🔑 the way you are; the way you do and say things
> **discouraged** *(adjective)* feeling bad or hopeless about something
> **expert** *(noun)* 🔑 a person who knows a lot about something
> **give up** *(phrasal verb)* to stop doing something
> **goal** *(noun)* 🔑 something that you want to do very much
> **lifestyle** *(noun)* the way that you live
> **pay attention** *(phrase)* to look, listen, or think about carefully

🔑 Oxford 2000 keywords

diet

1. Don't let your cough _____ a serious problem. Call your doctor today.

2. Toshi's _____ is to gain five pounds this month.

3. I want to _____ this diet, but my doctor says I need to lose 15 more pounds.

4. Dr. Park is a(n) _____ on food. He teaches food science at the university.

5. My brother eats well and exercises every day. He has a healthy _____.

6. Kate doesn't _____ to her health. She gets sick often.

7. The child's _____ in class is very bad. The teacher will talk with the parents about the problem.

8. I received a bad grade on my math quiz. I'm _____,

because I studied hard for the quiz.

 **B.** Go online for more practice with the vocabulary.

C. **PREVIEW** Quickly scan the excerpt to answer these questions.

1. What kinds of habits is this excerpt about?

2. How many "stages of change" are there?

D. **QUICK WRITE** Think about an unhealthy habit you have. Answer these questions. Use this section for your Unit Assignment.

1. What is your unhealthy habit? _____

2. Why is it an unhealthy habit? _____

3. Why is it hard to change this habit? _____

WORK WITH THE READING

A. Read the textbook excerpt and find information about changing unhealthy habits.

When Does a Change Become a Habit?

1   Everyone has a few unhealthy habits. For example, maybe you eat junk food[1] or drink a lot of coffee. Maybe you get too little sleep, or you never exercise. You know these habits aren't good for you. You should exercise more often, but you don't. Why? Because bad habits are very hard to change.

2   To change a habit, you have to change your **behavior**. It is always difficult at the beginning. But after some time, your new behavior **becomes** a new habit. **Experts** say that people need 20 to 70 days to change a habit. Some

habits can take a year to change. According to experts, there are six stages of change.

The Six Stages of Change

1. **Ignoring.** You ignore[2] the problem or don't **pay attention** to it. You don't want to believe that it's an unhealthy habit.

2. **Thinking.** You know your habit is unhealthy, but you don't have a plan to change it.

3. **Deciding.** You decide[3] to change your bad habit. You make a plan to change.

4. **Acting.** You start to change your unhealthy habit.

---

[1] **junk food:** food that is quick to prepare but is bad for your health

[2] **ignore:** to know something but not do anything about it
[3] **decide:** to think about and choose something

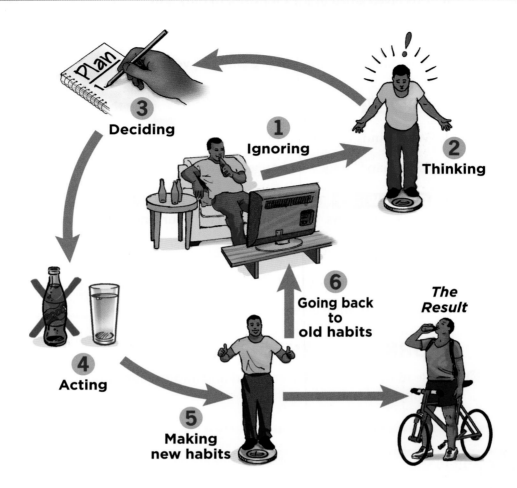

3 Deciding

1 Ignoring

2 Thinking

6 Going back to old habits

The Result

4 Acting

5 Making new habits

5. **Making new habits.** After many weeks, your new behavior becomes a new habit.

6. **Going back to old habits.** You go back to your old habit for a day, or a week, or a month. Don't be **discouraged**. This happens to everyone.

3   People usually want to change their bad habits quickly and easily. Remember, habits take a long time to make, so they take a long time to change. Most people aren't patient. In addition, they don't want to be uncomfortable. For instance, when you

start a diet, you feel hungry. If you begin an exercise program, you feel tired or sore. You will probably be uncomfortable when you change a habit, but don't **give up**. Think about your **goal**: a healthy **lifestyle**. With hard work, healthy behaviors can slowly become healthy habits.

4   Changing a habit isn't easy. It takes time, and you have to be patient. But the result is a healthier lifestyle and a happier you.

Tip for Success

To help you answer a question by scanning, underline important words in the question. Scanning for those words makes it easy to find the information.

B. Circle the answer that best completes each statement.

1. Most people don't change their habits because _____.
   a. it's hard to do
   b. they prefer to be unhealthy
   c. they don't know how

2. Most people need _____ to change a habit.
   a. about 20 days
   b. 20 to 70 days
   c. a year

3. _____ to their old habits.
   a. Many people return
   b. Few people return
   c. Everyone returns

4. When you first change your habit, you will probably _____.
   a. feel uncomfortable
   b. feel angry
   c. feel healthier

5. The main idea of the reading is that _____.
   a. it is too difficult to change bad habits
   b. you can change a habit if you are patient and remember your goal
   c. you will be healthier and happier if you change bad habits

C. Read the statements. Write *T* (true) or *F* (false). Then correct each false statement to make it true.

_____ 1. Most people have only one unhealthy habit.

_____ 2. It is unhealthy to eat junk food.

_____ 3. Some habits take a day to change.

_____ 4. At first it is easy to change your behavior.

_____ 5. It's important to have a goal.

_____ 6. People hardly ever return to old habits.

D. Read the sentences. What stage of change is each person at?

soda

1. James drinks several sodas every day. He doesn't believe soda is unhealthy.

   ignoring

2. Matt started exercising two months ago, but he hasn't done any exercise this week.

   _____

3. Isabel eats a lot of junk food. She knows it is unhealthy, but she keeps eating it.

   _____

4. Sun-Hee wants to get more exercise. She's going to start walking to work. She wants to start an exercise class, too.

   _____

5. Mary stopped drinking coffee two months ago. Now she drinks tea every morning.

   _____

6. Carlos started a diet this week. He's eating more fruits and vegetables.

   _____

Reading Skill	Identifying pronoun references

Pronouns replace nouns. Writers often use a pronoun after they introduce a noun. When you read a pronoun, ask yourself, "What does this pronoun refer to?"

Sarah drinks a lot of coffee. I think **it** makes **her** very nervous.

Dan's goal is to lose 10 pounds. **He** says he'll reach **it** in a month.

A. Read these sentences. What does the underlined pronoun refer to? Circle the words and draw an arrow.

1. To change a habit, you have (to change your behavior.) It is always difficult at the beginning.

2. You ignore the problem or don't pay attention to <u>it</u>.

3. You know your habit is unhealthy, but you don't have a plan to change <u>it</u>.

4. Remember, habits take a long time to make, so <u>they</u> take a long time to change.

5. Mauro loves playing video games. <u>He</u> can't stop playing <u>them</u>.

6. Mina's grades were low last semester. <u>Her</u> goal is to study more this semester.

 **B.** Go online for more practice with identifying pronoun references.

 # WRITE WHAT YOU THINK

A. Discuss these questions with a partner or in a group.

1. What habit do you want to change?

2. Why is it difficult to change this habit?

3. What can you do to change this habit?

B. Choose one question from Activity A and write an answer. Look back at your Quick Write on page 93. Think about what you learned.

Question: _____

My answer: _____

_____

_____

READING 2 | Dr. Lee on Health

You are going to read a newspaper article. A doctor answers questions from readers. Use the article to find information and ideas for your Unit Assignment.

PREVIEW THE READING

A. **VOCABULARY** Here are some words from Reading 2. Read the sentences. Circle the meaning of the <u>underlined</u> words.

1. I <u>am addicted to</u> coffee. When I don't drink coffee, I get a headache.
   a. like
   b. can't stop drinking

2. At the end of a long workday, Matt feels <u>exhausted</u>. He just wants to rest.
   a. extremely tired
   b. talkative

3. I have two tests this week. I feel a lot of <u>stress</u>.
   a. calm
   b. worry

Vocabulary Skill Review

In Unit 2, you learned about word families. What are some adjective forms of the word *stress*? What is the noun form of the word *create*?

4. I want to <u>break</u> my habit of drinking sodas. They have too much sugar.
   a. start
   b. stop

5. She drinks water <u>instead of</u> juice. Water is healthier.
   a. in addition to
   b. to replace

6. My friend is very heavy. He needs to <u>lose weight</u>.
   a. become thinner
   b. become heavier

7. I want to give you some money, but <u>unfortunately</u> I don't have any.
   a. sadly
   b. happily

8. When I cook, I don't use a recipe. I like to <u>create</u> my own dishes.
   a. name
   b. make

B. Go online for more practice with the vocabulary.

C. **PREVIEW** Scan the article for names. Complete the sentences.

1. _____ wants to lose weight.

2. _____ gives advice to readers.

3. _____ plays a lot of video games.

WORK WITH THE READING

A. Read the article to find information about changing unhealthy habits.

Dr. Lee on Health

Sleepless Sam

1 Dear Dr. Lee,

I am **addicted to** video games. I can't stop playing them. I don't feel tired at night because I love playing games. I usually stay up until 3 a.m. I never get enough sleep! During the day, I am **exhausted,** and I fall asleep in class. I feel a lot of **stress** because I am behind in my schoolwork. What's your advice?

Sleepless Sam

2 Dear Sam,

Your problem isn't unusual. Many people are addicted to video games. How can you **break** this habit? First, you should make a plan. Begin to make changes slowly. For example, if you usually play games five hours a day, you could play four hours a day for the first week. The next week, you could play three hours a day. Your goal should be one hour a day of video games. Second, replace video games with a different activity. You could spend time with friends **instead of** with video games. You could turn off your computer at 9:00 and read a good book. You will want to play video games, but you need to break this habit. Good luck!

Dr. Lee

3 Dear Dr. Lee,

I love the TV show *The Biggest Loser*. Contestants[1] on the show try to **lose weight**, and most of them are successful. They reach their goals. I want to lose 20 pounds (9 kilograms). Will the show's diet plan work for me?

Mary

4 Dear Mary,

The contestants on *The Biggest Loser* lose a lot of weight quickly. Diet and exercise experts plan everything the contestants eat and do. But what happens after the show? **Unfortunately**, most contestants gain weight again. Why? After the show, contestants don't exercise five to six hours a day. They often return to unhealthy lifestyles. If you want to lose weight, there are no quick and easy diet plans. It takes time to lose weight and learn new habits. You should **create** your own diet plan. Remember your goal: a healthy lifestyle.

Dr. Lee

The Biggest Loser

---

[1] **contestants:** people in a contest or game show

B. Circle the correct answer.

1. Sam is tired during the day because he ____.
   a. stays up late
   b. falls asleep in class
   c. feels a lot of stress
   d. doesn't drink coffee

2. Dr. Lee thinks that Sam should ____.
   a. get up early
   b. change his habit slowly
   c. play different games
   d. break his habit

3. Mary writes to Dr. Lee because she wants to ____.
   a. be on a TV program
   b. meet Dr. Lee
   c. lose weight
   d. gain weight

4. Dr. Lee says that Mary should ____.
   a. create her own diet plan
   b. go on the TV show
   c. lose 20 pounds
   d. not try to lose weight

C. Read the statements. Write _T_ (true) or _F_ (false). Then correct each false statement to make it true.

____ 1. Sam usually stays up until 2 a.m.

____ 2. Dr. Lee says Sam's goal should be to play video games for 30 minutes a day.

____ 3. The contestants lose weight quickly on the show.

____ 4. After the show, most contestants continue to exercise five to six hours a day.

____ 5. Dr. Lee believes that there are no quick and easy diet plans.

____ 6. Dr. Lee gives Mary tips and suggestions for her own diet plan.

D. Answer these questions.

1. Sam isn't tired at night. Why?

   _____

2. Why is Sam behind in his schoolwork?

   _____

3. According to Dr. Lee, does Sam have a common problem?

_____

4. What are the two suggestions for Sam?

_____

5. How much weight does Mary want to lose?

_____

6. Why do contestants gain weight after the TV program?

_____

7. Which answer do you think is the most helpful: Dr. Lee's reply to Sam or to Mary? Why?

_____

 **E.** Go online to read *Sleep Habits* and check your comprehension.

 ## WRITE WHAT YOU THINK

A. Discuss these questions with a partner or in a group. Look back at your Quick Write on page 99. Think about what you learned.

1. What unhealthy habit do you have? Why is it important to change the habit?

2. Do you have a goal? What is it?

3. Do you have a plan? What is it?

 B. Go online to watch the video about staying healthy. Then check your comprehension.

advice *(n.)* words that you say to help someone decide what to do

floss *(v.)* to use a special kind of string to clean between your teeth

increase *(v.)* to become bigger or more

results *(n.)* something that happens because of something else

VIDEO VOCABULARY

C. **Think about the unit video, Reading 1, and Reading 2 as you discuss these questions. Then choose one question and write an answer.**

1. In Reading 1, there are six stages of change. Think about the people in Reading 2. Which stage is Sam at? Which stage is Mary at?

2. Which habit in Reading 2 is harder to break? Why? In your opinion, how long will it take to change each habit?

Question: _____

My answer: _____

_____

_____

Building Vocabulary | Collocations

Collocations are words that we often use together. For example, we can use the verbs *gain* or *lose* with the noun *weight*:

- I often **gain weight** during the holidays.
- I usually **lose weight** during the summer.

Reduce and *lose* have similar meanings, but we don't say "I often reduce weight."

Verb + noun collocations

break a habit	It's hard to **break the habit** of eating junk food.
gain/lose weight	I want to **lose weight**.
set a goal	I **set a goal** to run a mile in ten minutes.
reach a goal	Next year, I will **reach my goal**. I will become a nurse.

Verb + preposition collocations

cut down on	I'm too heavy. I need to **cut down on** desserts.
be behind in	I **am behind in** my school work.
go off	Last weekend, I **went off** my diet. I had dessert every night.
go on	I **will go on** a new diet tomorrow.

A. Complete the sentences. Use words and collocations from the Building Vocabulary box on page 102.

My house is messy.

1. I will _____ to graduate from a four-year college.

2. I will _____ in about five years.

3. My doctor said I should _____. I am too heavy.

4. My house is messy. I am very busy this week, so I

   _____ my housecleaning chores.

5. I often fall asleep in front of the TV. I need to _____ that

   _____.

6. I'm going to _____ video games. I'll only play

   for an hour a day.

B. Answer these questions. Then ask and answer questions with a partner.

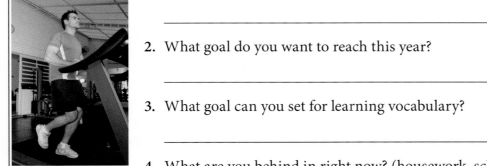

1. What habit do you want to break? What do you want to stop doing?

   _____

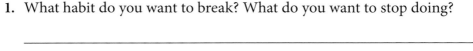

2. What goal do you want to reach this year?

   _____

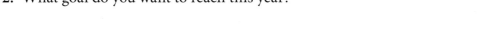

3. What goal can you set for learning vocabulary?

   _____

4. What are you behind in right now? (housework, schoolwork, email)

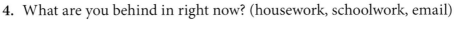

   _____

I will reach my goal.

C. Go online for more practice with collocations.

WRITING

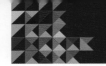

 **UNIT OBJECTIVE** ▶▶▶▶ **At the end of this unit, you are going to write about how to change an unhealthy habit. Your sentences will include information from the readings, the unit video, and your own ideas.**

Grammar | Modals *can*, *could*, and *should*

1. A modal comes before a base form verb. Modals can be affirmative or negative.*

> I **should eat** more fruit.   Sometimes I **can't sleep** at night.
> ⌐modal base verb   ⌐modal base verb

Don't put an *-s* at the end of the verb.

> ✓ Correct: He **can eat** a whole pizza.
> ✗ Incorrect: He can eats a whole pizza.

2. Use *can/can't* to talk about possibility or ability.

> Some habits **can** take a year to change.   She **can't** speak Arabic.

3. Use *could* to make a polite suggestion.

> You **could** come with me to my exercise class.

4. Use *should/shouldn't* to give advice.

> They **should** eat more fruit.   They **shouldn't** eat junk food.

*The full forms of *shouldn't* and *can't* are *should not* and *cannot*.

A. Read this paragraph from Reading 2. Underline the modals *could* or *should* + verb. Label each modal as *S* (Suggestion) or *A* (Advice).

    Many people are addicted to video games. How can you break this
                                 A
habit? First, you <u>should make</u> a plan. Begin to make changes slowly.
For example, if you usually play games five hours a day, you could play
four hours a day for the first week. The next week, you could play three
hours a day. Your goal should be one hour a day of video games. Second,
replace video games with a different activity. You could spend time with
friends instead of with video games. You could turn off your computer

at 9:00 and read a good book. You will want to play video games, but you need to break this habit. Good luck!

B. Complete these sentences with *can* or *can't*.

1. If I eat one potato chip, I _____ stop. I want to eat more.

2. It's difficult to break a habit, but you _____ do it.

3. People _____ become addicted to soda.

4. Most people _____ lose weight when they exercise every day.

5. I _____ speak loudly today. I have a bad cold.

C. Complete these sentences with *should* or *shouldn't*.

1. You _____ drink more than three cups of coffee a day.

2. It's very cold outside. You _____ wear a jacket.

3. It's really hot. We _____ go outside right now.

4. During class, you _____ pay attention to the teacher.

5. David _____ change his lifestyle. He needs to eat less junk food.

6. Anna feels a lot of stress. She _____ work so hard.

D. Read these statements. Write polite suggestions with *could*.

1. I'm having trouble with my homework.

   Suggestion: _You could ask your teacher for help._____

2. I need to gain weight.

   Suggestion: _____

3. I need to lose weight.

   Suggestion: _____

4. I need to relax.

   Suggestion: _____

E. Go online for more practice with modals *can*, *could*, and *should*.

F. Go online for the grammar expansion.

After you write, check your writing. A good way to check your writing is to use an editing checklist. This helps you remember common mistakes. When your writing has no mistakes, it is easy to read and understand.

Here is an editing checklist. Check your writing for each type of error (mistake).

		Editing Checklist
☐	1.	Capitalize the first word in a sentence or question. Capitalize proper nouns.
☐	2.	Use apostrophes ('), periods (.), and question marks (?) correctly.
☐	3.	Make sure every sentence has a subject and a verb. Make sure that subjects and verbs agree.
☐	4.	Check that you use vocabulary correctly.
☐	5.	Check words for correct spelling. Watch out for words that you often misspell.

Make your own editing checklist.

Put a star (✳) by the type of error you make most often.

Add words that you often misspell.

As you learn more English, add to your checklist.

A. Read each sentence. Find and correct the capitalization error(s).

   Dr. Wilson   I
1. ~~dr. wilson~~ says i should eat more fresh fruit.

2. my cousin is addicted to video games.

3. on monday sarah is going to give up smoking.

4. i am behind in my english class.

5. richard set a goal to climb mount shasta in july.

6. the lifestyle in the u.s. is very different from the lifestyle in china.

7. miss garcia is an expert in asian history.

8. the hospital is on the corner of mission street and state avenue.

Writing Tip

An apostrophe is used in contractions (*I'm, he's*) and to show possession (*Ahmed's, Ed's*). The contraction for *it is* is *it's*. The possessive for *it* is *its*. There is no apostrophe for the possessive.

B. Read each sentence. Add the missing apostrophes, periods, and question marks.

1. Could you please pay attention?

2. Marys goal is to get more sleep each night

3. Im not discouraged because I know losing weight will take a long time

4. Why are you so exhausted

5. The boys behavior shows that he has a lot of stress

6. Theyre going to create a plan for healthier meals

7. Are you addicted to your cell phone

8. Smoking is a very hard habit to break

C. Read each sentence. Correct each mistake with the subject or verb.

1. My grandmother is 75 years old, and she is very healthy.

2. Is very careful about her diet.

3. She never eat too much food.

4. She no gain weight.

5. She and her friend goes for a walk every morning.

6. Her daily habits keeps her healthy.

D. Find and correct the ten spelling errors.

1. unhelthy	6. behavior	11. creat
2. becoming	7. unfortunatly	12. expirt
3. habit	8. discoraged	13. quikly
4. lifestyle	9. lose weght	14. atention
5. exhasted	10. headace	15. should

E. Read the student paragraph. Use the Editing Checklist to find and correct the 11 errors. How many of each type of error are there? Write the numbers in the Editing Checklist.

My older Sister feel a lot of stress about school. She worry about her classes she thinks her grades are bad, but they very good. my sister studies every nite until midnight. I think she shold relax for a while every day. Do you think I shold tell her.

	Editing Checklist
___	1. Capitalize the first word in a sentence or question. Capitalize proper nouns.
___	2. Use apostrophes, periods, and question marks correctly.
___	3. Make sure every sentence has a subject and a verb. Make sure that subjects and verbs agree.
___	4. Check words for correct spelling.

F. Look at the student's errors in the Editing Checklist in Activity E. Answer the questions.

1. What is the most common error for this student?

2. What is the least common error for this student?

3. What words did the student misspell?

G. Rewrite the student's paragraph in Activity E. Correct all of the errors.

H. Look at some of your own writing. Make your own editing checklist by adding to the checklist above. Put a star (✲) next to your most common mistakes. Add words that you often misspell to the checklist.

 I. Go online for more practice with using an editing checklist.

 In this assignment, you are going to write about how to change an unhealthy habit. Think about the Unit Question, "How can you change an unhealthy habit?" Use the readings, the unit video, and your work in this unit. Look at the Self-Assessment checklist on page 110.

iQ ONLINE   Go to the Online Writing Tutor for a writing model and alternate Unit Assignments.

A. **BRAINSTORM** Read the text messages below. With a partner, discuss the two questions. For each question, think of several possible answers.

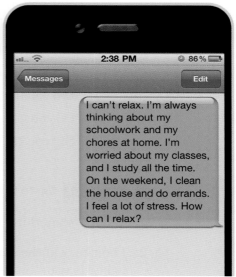

iQ ONLINE   **B.** **WRITE** Choose one question from Activity A. Answer with complete sentences. Use your **BRAINSTORM** notes to help you. Go to *iQ Online* to use the Online Writing Tutor.

C. REVISE Review your sentences with a partner. Read your partner's sentences. Then go online and use the Peer Review worksheet. Discuss the review with your partner.

D. EDIT AND REWRITE Complete the Self-Assessment checklist. Make final changes to your sentences. Be prepared to hand in your work or discuss it in class.

Yes	No	SELF-ASSESSMENT
☐	☐	Do you use collocations correctly?
☐	☐	Do you use the modals *can*, *could*, and *should* correctly to give suggestions and advice?
☐	☐	Do you use vocabulary from the unit?
☐	☐	Did you capitalize the first word in each sentence?
☐	☐	Did you capitalize proper nouns?
☐	☐	Did you use apostrophes, periods, and question marks correctly?
☐	☐	Do your subjects and verbs agree?
☐	☐	Did you check your spelling?

E. REFLECT Go to the Online Discussion Board to discuss these questions.

1. What is something new you learned in this unit?

2. Look back at the Unit Question—How can you change an unhealthy habit? Is your answer different now than when you started the unit? If yes, how is it different?

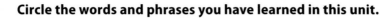

TRACK YOUR SUCCESS

Circle the words and phrases you have learned in this unit.

Nouns
behavior 🔑
expert 🔑 AWL
goal 🔑 AWL
habit 🔑
lifestyle
stress 🔑 AWL

Verbs
become 🔑
break 🔑
create 🔑 AWL

Adjectives
discouraged
exhausted
unhealthy

Adverb
unfortunately 🔑

Preposition
instead (of) 🔑

Phrases/Collocations
be addicted (to)
be behind in
break a habit
cut down on (dessert)
gain weight
give up
go off (a diet)
go on (a diet)
lose weight
pay attention
reach a goal
set a goal

🔑 Oxford 2000 keywords
AWL Academic Word List

Check (✓) the skills you learned. If you need more work on a skill, refer to the page(s) in parentheses.

READING ■	I can identify pronoun references. (p. 96)
VOCABULARY ■	I can use collocations. (p. 102)
GRAMMAR ■	I can use modals *can*, *could*, and *should*. (p. 104)
WRITING ■	I can use an editing checklist. (p. 106)
UNIT OBJECTIVE ▶▶▶▶ ■	I can find information and ideas to write about how to change an unhealthy habit.

UNIT 7

Urban Planning

READING ▶	building reading fluency
VOCABULARY ▶	word families
GRAMMAR ▶	past of *be*; simple past affirmative statements
WRITING ▶	identifying fragments and complete sentences

UNIT QUESTION

Why do people live in cities?

A What words describe your city or town? Circle three words from the box. Compare your answers with your classmates.

beautiful	dirty	inexpensive
boring	exciting	quiet
busy	expensive	safe
clean	friendly	ugly

UNIT
OBJECTIVE ▶▶▶▶ Read an article from a business journal and a blog post.
Find information and ideas to describe a city and what
people enjoy about it.

◗ **B** Listen to *The Q Classroom* online. Then answer
these questions.

1. What did the students say?

2. How is their city different from your city or town?
For example, does your city or town have good
public transportation?

iQ ONLINE **C** Go online to watch the video about people living
in cities. Then check your comprehension.

VIDEO VOCABULARY

crowded *(adj.)* full of people

garbage *(n.)* things that you do not
want any more; waste material

healthy *(adj.)* well; not often sick

produce *(n.)* food that you grow on a
farm or in a garden to sell

iQ ONLINE **D** Go to the Online Discussion Board
to discuss the Unit Question with
your classmates.

READING 1 | Why Do People Love Their Cities?

You are going to read an article from a business journal about why people love their cities. Use the article to find information and ideas for your Unit Assignment.

PREVIEW THE READING

A. **VOCABULARY** Here are some words from Reading 1. Read each sentence. Then write each <u>underlined</u> word next to the correct definition.

1. The newspaper did a <u>survey</u> about the city's schools. They interviewed about 20,000 people.

2. One <u>characteristic</u> of a good city is friendly people.

3. Two men robbed a bank and took a lot of money. It was a serious <u>crime</u>.

4. The <u>economy</u> in my city is good. There are many jobs, and the stores are full of customers.

5. There are about 55 <u>residents</u> in my apartment building.

6. Trains, buses, and subways are part of the <u>public</u> transportation in the city.

7. People in this small town <u>welcome</u> visitors. They enjoy showing visitors their town.

8. My grandfather is an <u>immigrant</u> from China. He was born in China. Now he lives in Canada.

a resident of an apartment building

a. _____ (*noun*) something that is against the law

b. _____ (*adjective*) for everyone

c. _____ (*verb*) to be friendly when someone arrives

d. _____ (*noun*) a special quality that makes a person or thing different from others

e. _____ (*noun*) a person who comes to another country to live there

f. _____ (*noun*) money and business in a place (city, country, world)

g. _____ (*noun*) people who live in a place

h. _____ (*noun*) a list of questions about a topic

 B. Go online for more practice with the vocabulary.

⚷ Oxford 2000 keywords

C. **PREVIEW** This article is about characteristics of great cities. Which characteristics are important to you? Number the characteristics from 1 (most important) to 6 (least important).

___ lots of parks

___ good schools and colleges

___ good jobs

___ good public transportation

___ nice, inexpensive apartments and houses

___ fun entertainment and events

D. **QUICK WRITE** Think about a city that you know. Answer these questions. Use this section for your Unit Assignment.

1. What is the city? Where is it located? _____

2. What do you like about the city? _____

3. What do you like to do there? _____

WORK WITH THE READING

A. Read the article from a business journal. Find information about why people love their cities.

Why Do People Love Their Cities?

1   What is the best city in the world? Every year, Mercer Consulting does a **survey** of over 400 cities around the world. They look at ten **characteristics** of cities, including **crime**, the **economy**, the cost of housing, and more. In 2014, they reported that Vienna, Austria, was the best city in the world. Other great cities were Zurich, Switzerland; Auckland, New Zealand; Munich, Germany; and Vancouver, Canada.

2   When **residents** love their city, the city grows and the economy improves. The Mercer study is interesting, but it doesn't answer this question:

Vienna, Austria

Zurich, Switzerland

Marienplatz, a central plaza in Munich, Germany

Auckland, New Zealand

Why do residents love their cities? Many city leaders around the world wanted an answer to this question. In 2008, Gallup and the Knight Foundation started a new survey to answer it. They interviewed 43,000 adults in 25 cities in the United States. Experts found three important answers to the question. These three answers were the same in all 25 cities.

Places for social activities

3   Restaurants, museums, and community events are all places for social activities. Residents can enjoy spending time with friends and family members in the city. In addition, **public** spaces are important. Public spaces can be parks, plazas, and downtown areas. In public spaces, residents can sit, eat lunch, relax, or meet with friends.

Beauty

4   The appearance of a city is very important. Parks, trees, and flowers add beauty to a city.

Openness

5   Openness means the friendliness of a city. Does the city **welcome** new residents? Does it welcome **immigrants** from other countries? Does it welcome people of different ages and interests?

6   When residents love their city, the city economy grows. When the economy grows, there are more jobs. But jobs are not the most important thing for residents. They do not love their city because of good jobs, good highways, or good schools. They love their cities because of places for social activities, beauty, and openness. City leaders should pay attention to these characteristics in their cities.

B. Read each sentence. Where can you find this information in the article? Write the paragraph number.

_____ a.   A survey asked: Why do residents love their cities?

_____ b.   Residents like a welcoming city.

_____ c.   Social activities are important to residents.

_____ d.   Good highways don't make a city great.

_____ e.   Mercer Consulting looks for the best city in the world each year.

_____ f.   They interviewed 43,000 adults.

_____ g.   Vienna was the best city in 2014.

_____ h.   City leaders should make sure their city has places for social activities, beauty, and openness.

C. Look at Activity B. Which sentences are main ideas? Which are supporting ideas? Write the letters.

1. Main ideas: _____

_____

2. Supporting ideas: _____

_____

D. Circle the correct response.

1. The Mercer Consulting survey included more than ____ .
   a. 43,000 cities
   b. 400 cities
   c. 2,014 cities

2. Crime, the economy, and the cost of housing are important ____ .
   a. problems
   b. characteristics
   c. activities

3. The city grows and the economy improves when residents ____ .
   a. love their city
   b. work hard
   c. use public transportation

4. The Mercer study could not say why ____ .
   a. a city's economy improves
   b. cities grow
   c. people love their cities

5. The three most important characteristics of cities are: ____ .
   a. restaurants, museums, and community events
   b. places for social activities, beauty, and openness
   c. people of different ages, interests, and national backgrounds

E. Answer these questions with information from the article.

1. Which city is the best in the world? _____

2. What do people do in public spaces? _____

   _____

3. What can add beauty to a city? _____

4. What does openness mean? _____

   _____

iQ ONLINE **F. Go online to read *Exploring Pompeii* and check your comprehension.**

WRITE WHAT YOU THINK

A. With a partner, write three cities or towns in the chart. Then give each city a number from 1 to 5 (1 = very bad, 5 = very good) for each characteristic in the chart.

Critical Thinking **Tip**

Activity A asks you to **evaluate** different cities. When you evaluate, you use information and opinions to make decisions about things.

City or town:			
Places for social activities			
Beauty			
Openness			

B. Which of the cities do you like the best? Why? Number your favorites from 1 to 3. Look back at your Quick Write on page 115. Is that city better than these? Why or why not?

shopping in Malmö, Sweden

Inokashira Park, Tokyo, Japan

a film festival in Bryant Park, New York City

Reading Skill | Building reading fluency

Reading fluency means how quickly and easily you read. It is important to increase your reading speed. Here are two ways to build your reading fluency.

1. Move your eyes across each line and down the article. Keep your eyes moving. Don't stop for words you don't know.

2. Remember: You don't have to understand every word in an article.

    • The first time you read, look for the main ideas.
    • The second time you read, pay more attention to the details and the vocabulary.

Sometimes you need to read an article three or four times. Each time, try to read it more quickly. When you read something several times, you can increase your reading fluency.

A. Do three timed readings of Reading 1 on pages 115–116. Each time, read for 30 seconds. Follow these steps.

1. When your teacher says "Start," read from the beginning of Reading 1.

2. When your teacher says "Stop," write a small *1* exactly where you stop.

3. Do the timed reading two more times. Each time, start at the beginning. The second time, write a *2* where you stop. The third time, write a *3*.

4. Did you read more each time? Did you increase your reading fluency?

B. Nine words are missing from this paragraph, but you don't need them to understand the main ideas. Read the paragraph without stopping. Then circle the correct answers below.

Residents of a city are interested in the _____ of life in a city. They want to live happily and _____ in a city. For example, places for social activities and events, public areas and parks, natural beauty, and openness are all important for residents. But tourists are _____ in different things. Tourists want to see _____ things such as _____ monuments and famous places. They want to experience the most _____ places in a city. Easy transportation, friendly people, and _____ experiences are all important to tourists. For this _____, cities with the best lifestyle are not always the top tourist cities. And the top tourist _____ are not always the best places to live.

1. This article discusses ____.
   a. residents
   b. tourists and residents
   c. residents and friendly people
   d. immigrants

2. Residents and tourists are interested in ____ things in a city.
   a. the same
   b. famous
   c. different
   d. fun

3. The city with the best lifestyle is ____ the top tourist city.
   a. usually
   b. always
   c. never
   d. not always

 C. Go online for more practice with building reading fluency.

Prague, Czech Republic

You are going to read a blog post about readers' first impressions of Berlin, Germany. Use the blog post to find information and ideas for your Unit Assignment.

PREVIEW THE READING

Vocabulary Skill Review

In Unit 6, you learned that collocations are words that we often use together. What are some collocations with the words *international*, *impression*, and *opinion*?

A. **VOCABULARY** Here are some words from Reading 2. Read the sentences. Circle the correct meaning of the underlined words.

1. There are many <u>complaints</u> about this restaurant. The food is not very good.
   a. comments from unhappy people
   b. comments from happy people

2. In my <u>opinion</u>, the city lifestyle is wonderful and exciting.
   a. a thought about something
   b. a report about a topic

3. There are many <u>international</u> students at this university.
   a. from different countries
   b. intelligent

4. This park <u>seems</u> very safe. There are a lot of families with children.
   a. looks like it is
   b. smells like it is

5. The air in the city is dirty and polluted. It needs to <u>improve</u>.
   a. get worse
   b. get better

6. My first <u>impression</u> of the neighborhood was good. I liked it because there were many beautiful trees.
   a. idea or feeling
   b. town or city

7. On weekends, I buy fresh fruit at a farmers' <u>market</u> downtown. Each farmer sells a good variety of fruits.
   a. place to eat food
   b. place to shop for things

8. This museum is very expensive. I'm <u>surprised</u>. I thought it was free.
   a. serious feeling about something
   b. feeling when something unusual happens

iQ ONLINE **B.** Go online for more practice with the vocabulary.

C. **PREVIEW** With a partner, talk about Berlin, Germany. Together, make a list of everything you know about Berlin.

D. **QUICK WRITE** Why do you think some people may enjoy living in Berlin? Write a list. Use this section for your Unit Assignment.

WORK WITH THE READING

A. Read the blog post. Find information about why people live in cities.

First Impressions

1   Some long-time residents of Berlin have **complaints** about their city. Last week, we invited some of our newer residents to give their thoughts and **opinions**.

Mei

2   I am from Taiwan, and I moved here two years ago. I'm studying engineering at Humboldt University. Berlin is very **international**. That is its best characteristic. There are students and professors from all over the world. During my first year here, many students didn't **seem** friendly toward new people. I was shy at the beginning because my German wasn't very good. When my German **improved**, I tried to talk to other students more. After several months, I made a few good friends. Then I started to enjoy the city with my friends. My first **impression** was not very good. People seemed unfriendly. But now I have a good opinion of Berlin, and I enjoy studying here.

Humboldt University

Tala

3   I am from the Philippines, and I moved here with my family five years ago. I really don't like cold weather, so at first, I was unhappy. But people in this city don't stay inside in the winter. For example, last December, I visited the outdoor **markets** with my parents. It was cold, and it was dark at 3:30 p.m. But the markets were so colorful! My family and I walked around for hours.

outdoor café

We went to many shops. We enjoyed the beautiful lights. Everyone was outside, having fun! When we were too cold, we stopped for a hot drink at a café. Later in the evening, there was a free event. On that winter night, the city was exciting. The next day, I went ice skating with my friends. From the big outside skating rink, there was a beautiful view of the city. Now I think differently about the cold winter months.

Pedro

4   My first impression of Berlin was very good. This city really welcomes bicyclists, and that is very unusual. I love biking, but it can be dangerous in a city. On my first weekend in Berlin, I biked all over the city. There are special red bike paths everywhere, and they are very safe. I was really **surprised**. Also, I explored the beautiful city parks and gardens.

red bike paths in Berlin

B. Read the statements. Write *T* (true) or *F* (false). Then correct each false statement to make it true.

____ 1.   Mei moved to Berlin five years ago.

____ 2.   Mei didn't speak German very well when she arrived.

____ 3.   Mei doesn't like studying in Berlin now.

____ 4.   Residents of Berlin enjoy spending time outside in the winter.

____ 5.   Tala didn't like the outdoor markets.

____ 6.   Tala enjoyed skiing in Berlin.

____ 7.   Pedro enjoys running in the city parks in Berlin.

____ 8.   The bike paths in Berlin are red.

C. Fill in the chart. How does each person's impression of Berlin change? Then answer the questions on page 124.

	First impression	Later impression
Mei	Students weren't friendly.	
Tala	She didn't like the cold weather.	
Pedro		He still feels the same.

1. Which person had a very good first impression? Why?

2. For the other two people, what happened to change their impressions?

D. Answer these questions.

1. What did you learn about Berlin? Write three things.

   _____

2. At first, Mei's impression of Berlin was not very good. Why do you think that was?

   _____

3. Do you think you would enjoy visiting the outdoor markets in winter? Why or why not?

   _____

4. How is Berlin similar to your city?

   _____

5. How is Berlin different from your city?

   _____

 WRITE WHAT YOU THINK

A. Imagine that Mei, Tala, and Pedro are coming to your city or town. Complete the chart. Then discuss your answers with a partner.

Mei should see... because...   I can take her to...

	Where should you take this visitor?	What can you show your visitor? Why?
Mei		
Tala		
Pedro		

B. Discuss these questions with a partner or in a group. Look back at your Quick Write on page 122. Think about what you learned.

1. Why do people like to live in Berlin?

2. What would you enjoy in Berlin? Why?

C. Think about the unit video, Reading 1, and Reading 2 as you discuss these questions. Then choose one question and write an answer.

1. Think about the three characteristics of a good city. Which characteristic is the most important to you? Why?

2. In your opinion, how can your city improve? What does it need to do? Give examples and suggestions.

Question: _____

My answer: _____

_____

_____

_____

Building Vocabulary   Word families

pollution

When you learn a new word, use your dictionary to learn other words in the same **word family**. For example, look up *pollution* in your dictionary. You will find the verb *pollute* above it. To review word families, see Unit 2, page 25.

pol·lute /pəˈlut/ *verb* (**pol·lutes, pol·lut·ing, pol·lut·ed**)
to make the air, rivers, etc. dirty and dangerous: *Many of our rivers are polluted with chemicals from factories.*

pol·lu·tion 🔑 /pəˈluʃn/ *noun* [noncount]
1 the action of making the air, rivers, etc. dirty and dangerous: *We must stop the **pollution of** our beaches.*
2 dirty and dangerous chemicals, gases, etc. that harm the environment: *Our rivers are full of pollution.* ⊃ Look at the note at **environment**.

All dictionary entries are from the *Oxford Basic American Dictionary for learners of English.* © Oxford University Press 2011.

A. Complete the chart. Use your dictionary. (An X means that a word doesn't exist or that you don't need to know it.)

	Noun	Verb	Adjective
1.		appear	X
2.			interesting; interested
3.	X		modern
4.		X	public
5.	pollution		
6.			relaxing; relaxed
7.		X	safe
8.	society		social

a city library

B. Complete these sentences. Use the correct noun, verb, or adjective from Activity A. More than one answer may be correct.

1. I like to _____ relax _____ in the park. It is a _____ place.

2. Cars _____ the air and make it dirty. Cars cause

    _____ in the city.

3. The post office and the library are _____ buildings. Those

    buildings are open to the _____ six days a week.

4. Our airport is very old. Next year, the city will _____ it

    with free Internet service, new furniture, and new shops.

5. I'm a very talkative and _____ person. I like to

    _____ with my friends in the cafeteria after class.

6. I live in a very _____ neighborhood. I don't worry about

    my _____.

 C. Go online for more practice with word families.

WRITING

At the end of this unit, you are going to write about a city and what people enjoy about it. Your sentences will include information from the readings, the unit video, and your own ideas.

Grammar   Past of *be*; Simple past affirmative statements

Past of *be*

Use the past of *be* to identify and describe people and things in the past.

Affirmative and negative statements

subject	be	(not)	
I	**was**		happy in Hong Kong.
You We They	**were**	**(not)**	at the outdoor market.
He She It	**was**		in the public garden.

- You can contract negative statements:

  was not = wasn't   were not = weren't

Yes/No questions			Short answers		
be	subject		*yes*		*no*
Was	the apartment	expensive?	Yes, it **was**.		No, it **wasn't**.
Were	the streets	safe?	Yes, they **were**.		No, they **weren't**.

Information questions				Answers
wh- word	*be*	subject		
Who	**was**	the writer?		Charles Dickens **was** the writer.
What	**were**	the questions	about?	They **were** about cities.
Where	**was**	the museum?		It **was** near the park.

Simple past affirmative statements

The simple past describes completed actions in the past.

The simple past verb form is the same for all subjects.

> Last summer, we **visited** Miami.
> My cousins **welcomed** us into their home.
> The train **stopped** at the station.
> Ana **stayed** home and **studied** for the test.

Spelling of simple past verbs	
Add -*ed* after most verbs. Add -*d* after verbs that end in -*e*.	travel**ed**, walk**ed** welcome**d**, improve**d**
If a <u>one-syllable</u> verb ends in vowel + consonant, double the consonant and add -*ed*.	plan**ned**, stop**ped**
If the verb ends in a consonant + -*y*, change the *y* to *i* and add -*ed*.	stud**ied**, tr**ied**
If the verb ends in a vowel + -*y*, add -*ed*.	play**ed**, stay**ed**

The sky was very clear.

A. Complete each sentence with *was*, *were*, *wasn't*, or *weren't*.

1. The city _____was_____ very clean. There _____ any trash in the streets.

2. The sky _____ clear and blue. The air _____ polluted.

3. The taxi _____ very expensive. Next time, I will take a bus.

4. The residents _____ worried about crime. The city was very safe.

5. We _____ exhausted after the trip. The roads _____ very crowded, and traffic moved slowly.

6. Last year, the economy in my area _____ very bad.

7. I _____ happy about my new office. It was very dark.

B. Complete the two paragraphs about Dubai.

This first paragraph is a general description of Dubai. Use the simple present.

Dubai _____ (be) a very impressive, modern city. It
               1

_____ (have) some of the tallest buildings in the world,
    2

and the shopping malls, hotels, and restaurants _____ (be)
             3

all very new—and expensive! Dubai _____ (be) on a
             4

peninsula, and it _____ (have) beautiful beaches. The
          5

weather _____ (be) very sunny and warm.
     6

Dubai, United Arab Emirates

This paragraph is about the writer's first impressions of Dubai. Use the simple past.

My wife and I _____ (move) to Dubai in the United
          7

Arab Emirates last year. My first impression of Dubai _____ (be)
            8

good. The people _____ (be) very welcoming and
        9

_____ (answer) our questions. On the weekend, we
    10

_____ (walk) down narrow streets in the old market area.
    11

However, the daytime temperatures _____ (be) very hot. I
            12

_____ (try) to stay inside with the air conditioning.
    13

C. Put the words in the correct order to make questions. Then ask and answer the questions with a partner.

1. hot / it / was / yesterday ?

_____

2. people / were / friendly ?

_____

3. school building / last night / was / the / open ?

_____

4. your teacher / who / last year / was ?

_____

ONLINE

D. Go online for more practice with the past of *be* and simple past affirmative statements.

E. Go online for the grammar expansion.

Writing Skill | Identifying fragments and complete sentences

A **complete sentence** needs a subject and a verb. The subject is who or what the sentence is about. The verb tells what the subject does or what the subject thinks, feels, or is. To review simple sentences, see Unit 1, page 13.

The city is old and beautiful.
subject verb

The residents enjoy their city parks.
subject verb

A sentence with no subject or no verb is not complete. It is a **sentence fragment**.

✓ **She** is interested in history.
✗ Is interested in history. (no subject)

✓ The residents **relaxed** in the park.
✗ The residents in the park. (no verb)

Always check your writing and ask, *Does the sentence have a subject? Does the sentence have a verb?* Identify and correct any sentence fragments.

A. Read the sentences about the city of Boston. Underline the subjects and circle the verbs. Some sentences may have more than one subject or more than one verb.

1. My family and I went to Boston four years ago.

2. Boston is a very historic city.

3. We visited many historic buildings in the downtown area.

4. My family and I went to the famous public gardens and walked around.

5. We saw Quincy Market and had lunch there.

6. We watched sailboats on the Charles River.

B. Read each sentence. Write *C* if it is a complete sentence or *F* if it is a fragment.

____ 1.   The city very modern with some fantastic skyscrapers.

____ 2.   It has a strong economy and good public transportation.

____ 3.   The pollution not too bad during my visit last year.

____ 4.   Enjoyed going to the farmers market.

____ 5.   The city seemed very safe and relaxing.

____ 6.   After lunch, went to the new art museum.

____ 7.   The shopping in the city was really fantastic.

C. Correct the fragments in Activity B. Choose a subject or a verb from the box to make complete sentences.

I	is	my friends and I	was	we

1. _____

2. _____

3. _____

4. _____

 D. Go online for more practice with identifying fragments and complete sentences.

 **Write about a city**

 In this assignment, you are going to write about a city and what people enjoy about it. Think about the Unit Question, "Why do people live in cities?" Use the readings, the unit video, and your work in this unit. Look at the Self-Assessment checklist on page 132.

 Go to the Online Writing Tutor for a writing model and alternate Unit Assignments.

A. BRAINSTORM Think about a city you visited. Complete the T-chart below. Then share your ideas with a partner.

Places, parks, and shops in the city	Adjectives to describe the city

B. WRITE Answer the questions. Write several sentences for each question. Use your **BRAINSTORM** chart and notes to help you. Go to *iQ Online* to use the Online Writing Tutor.

1. When did you visit the city? Who did you go with?

2. What did you see or do?

3. What was the most interesting thing about the city?

4. Do you think this is a good city to live in? Explain your answer.

C. REVISE Review your sentences with a partner. Read your partner's sentences. Then go online and use the Peer Review worksheet. Discuss the review with your partner.

D. EDIT AND REWRITE Complete the Self-Assessment checklist. Make final changes to your sentences. Be prepared to hand in your work or discuss it in class.

SELF-ASSESSMENT		
Yes	No	
☐	☐	Does every sentence have a subject and a verb?
☐	☐	Do you write in complete sentences?
☐	☐	Do you use the correct form of vocabulary words from this unit?
☐	☐	Do you use the simple past correctly?

1. What is something new you learned in this unit?

2. Look back at the Unit Question—Why do people live in cities? Is your answer different now than when you started the unit? If yes, how is it different?

TRACK YOUR SUCCESS

Circle the words you have learned in this unit.

Nouns
appearance 🔑
beauty 🔑
characteristic 🔑
complaint 🔑
crime 🔑
economy 🔑 AWL
immigrant AWL
impression 🔑
interest 🔑
market 🔑
opinion 🔑
pollution 🔑

public 🔑
relaxation AWL
resident AWL
safety 🔑
society 🔑
survey AWL

Verbs
appear 🔑
improve 🔑
interest 🔑
modernize
pollute
relax 🔑 AWL
seem 🔑

socialize
welcome 🔑

Adjectives
interested 🔑
interesting 🔑
international 🔑
polluted
public 🔑
relaxed 🔑 AWL
relaxing 🔑 AWL
safe 🔑
social 🔑
surprised 🔑

🔑 Oxford 2000 keywords
AWL Academic Word List

Check (✓) the skills you learned. If you need more work on a skill, refer to the page(s) in parentheses.

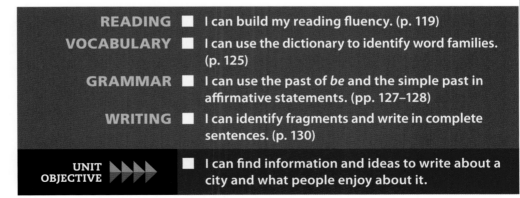

READING ■	I can build my reading fluency. (p. 119)
VOCABULARY ■	I can use the dictionary to identify word families. (p. 125)
GRAMMAR ■	I can use the past of *be* and the simple past in affirmative statements. (pp. 127–128)
WRITING ■	I can identify fragments and write in complete sentences. (p. 130)
UNIT OBJECTIVE ▶▶▶▶ ■	I can find information and ideas to write about a city and what people enjoy about it.

READING ▶ review: building reading fluency
VOCABULARY ▶ using the dictionary
GRAMMAR ▶ simple past with regular and irregular verbs
WRITING ▶ sentences with *and*

UNIT QUESTION

What events change our lives?

A Look at these important life events. In what order do they usually happen? Number them from 1 to 8. Discuss your answers with a partner.

____ get a job

____ get married

____ graduate from university

____ graduate from high school

____ move away from home

____ start school

____ buy a home

____ start a family

B Listen to *The Q Classroom* online. Then answer these questions.

1. What events does each person talk about?

2. What are some other events that change our lives?

 C Go to the Online Discussion Board to discuss the Unit Question with your classmates.

UNIT
OBJECTIVE ▶▶▶▶ Read an article from a business journal and an article from a sports magazine. Find information and ideas to write about an important event in your life.

135

READING

READING 1 | A Promise to Children

UNIT OBJECTIVE ▶▶▶▶
You are going to read an article from a business journal. The article is about a man named John Wood. Use the article to find information and ideas for your Unit Assignment.

PREVIEW THE READING

A. **VOCABULARY** Here are some words from Reading 1. Read the definitions. Then complete the sentences below.

---

continue *(verb)* 🔑 to not stop doing something

decide *(verb)* 🔑 to choose

dream *(noun)* 🔑 something good that you hope for

even *(adverb)* 🔑 used to show something surprising

opportunity *(noun)* 🔑 a chance to do something

organization *(noun)* 🔑 a group of people—they work together to meet a goal

promise *(verb)* 🔑 to say that you will do or will not do something

---

🔑 Oxford 2000 keywords

1. Can you loan me a little money? I _____ to pay you back tomorrow.

2. Did you _____ to take a trip? When do you need to make your decision?

3. Immigrants first came to the United States hundreds of years ago. Today, immigrants _____ to move to the United States.

4. Hassan's _____ is to become a restaurant owner someday.

5. I belong to a neighborhood _____. We meet once a month to talk about problems in our community.

6. _____ in winter, Dubai is sometimes very hot.

7. When I was young, I enjoyed working at my father's store. It wasn't hard, but I learned a lot about business. It was a great _____ for me.

iQ ONLINE **B.** Go online for more practice with the vocabulary.

C. PREVIEW Look at the photos and read the captions. Then answer the question.

What do you think John Wood did? Check (✓) your answer.
☐ a. He became a farmer in Nepal.
☐ b. He gave books to children in Nepal.
☐ c. He helped sick people in Nepal.

D. QUICK WRITE Answer these questions. Use this section for your Unit Assignment.

1. What is an important life event for a young child? _____

_____

2. What is an important life event for a teenager? _____

_____

3. What is an important life event for an older person? _____

_____

| Skill Review | Building reading fluency |

Remember: You can increase your reading speed. Read an article several times. The first time, read for the main idea. The second time, read for details. The third time, increase your reading fluency. Don't stop for new words. Review the Reading Skill box in Unit 7, page 119.

A. Read the article and find information about what events change our lives.

A Promise to Children

Before 1999, John Wood was a successful businessman. But that year, John Wood made a **promise**, and it changed his life completely.

1   In 1998, John Wood was an executive at Microsoft in Australia. He was only 35 years old, but he had an important job with a high salary and long hours. He needed a vacation, so he went hiking for three weeks in the Himalayan Mountains in Nepal. During his hike, he met a teacher from a small village. The teacher invited Wood on a tour of his school, and Wood was shocked[1]. There

John Wood in Nepal

Kathmandu Valley, Himalayas, Nepal

were only 20 books for hundreds of students, but they were not textbooks. They were tour books and novels[2] from other hikers. As Wood left the village, the school principal said: "Perhaps, sir, you will someday come back with books."

2   The visit to the village changed Wood, and he made a promise to himself: return to Nepal with books. He started to ask his friends and family for help. Later in 1998, Microsoft moved Wood to a job in China. **Even** in China, he **continued** to think about Nepal and collect books. In 1999, Wood and his father brought thousands of books to the village. In the same year, Wood **decided** to leave his job at Microsoft. He was a successful businessman, but

his new **dream** was to bring books and education to children around the world. He wanted all children to have the **opportunity** to be successful like him. In 2000, he started an **organization**, Room to Read.

3   At first, it was challenging[3]. He had no salary, and the organization's office was in his home. He had to raise a lot of money and hire good people. But Wood had strong business skills, and he was very organized. Many people became excited about Wood's dream, and Room to Read grew quickly.

4   In the first ten years, Room to Read helped five million children and built more than 1,000 schools and 11,000 libraries in Bangladesh, Cambodia, India, Laos, Nepal, South Africa, Sri Lanka, Vietnam, and Zambia. Also, the organization gave away more than nine million books and created hundreds of children's books in 23 languages. Today, Wood and Room to Read continue to help children in Asia and Africa. Their goal is to help educate millions of children around the world. Wood also published his first children's book in 2010, *Zak the Yak with Books on His Back*. Where does the story take place? You guessed it—Nepal.

---

[1] **shocked:** feeling surprised in a bad way
[2] **novel:** a written story about people and events that are not real

[3] **challenging:** difficult

B. Answer these questions.

1. Why did Wood go to Nepal in 1998?

   _____

2. How long was he there? _____

3. He visited a small village school. What did the school have?

   _____

4. Wood made a promise to return with books. Who did he promise?

   _____

5. Who helped Wood bring the first books to the village?

   _____

6. Why was Room to Read difficult for Wood?

   _____

C. Read the statements. Write *T* (true) or *F* (false). Then correct each false statement to make it true.

____ 1. John Wood worked at Microsoft in 1998.

   _____

____ 2. He moved to Nepal for work.

   _____

____ 3. He visited a school in Nepal, and it had many books.

   _____

____ 4. Wood decided to bring books and education to children.

   _____

____ 5. When he started Room to Read, Wood got a large salary.

   _____

____ 6. Room to Read built more than 11,000 schools in the first ten years.

   _____

Critical Thinking **Tip**

In Activity D, you complete a timeline of events. A **timeline** can help you organize and remember the order of important events.

D. Complete the timeline. Write the letter of each event in the correct place.

a. returned to Nepal with thousands of books   d. left his job at Microsoft

b. wrote a children's book   e. started Room to Read

c. went hiking in Nepal   f. moved to a job in China

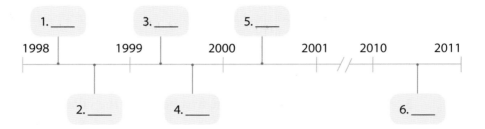

1. ____
3. ____
5. ____

1998   1999   2000   2001   2010   2011

2. ____
4. ____
6. ____

E. What event changed Wood's life in 1998? How do you think this changed the lives of children in villages in Asia and Africa?

WRITE WHAT YOU THINK

A. Which events happened in your life? Check (✓) the boxes. Then compare with a partner.

☐ was on a winning sports team   ☐ had an accident

☐ bought something very expensive   ☐ graduated from high school

☐ met an important or special person   ☐ applied to college

☐ experienced extreme weather   ☐ attended a different school

☐ visited a different country   ☐ moved to a different home

a winning team

B. Think about the Unit Question, "What events change our lives?" Discuss the questions in a group.

1. Which event changed your life?

2. When did this event happen?

3. How did it change your life?

C. Choose one question from Activity B and write an answer. Look back at your Quick Write on page 137. Think about what you learned.

You are going to read an article from a sports magazine. The article is about a basketball coach. Use the article to find information and ideas for your Unit Assignment.

PREVIEW THE READING

A. **VOCABULARY** **Here are some words from Reading 2. Read each sentence. Then write each <u>underlined</u> word next to the correct definition.**

a garage

Vocabulary Skill Review

In Unit 7, you learned to use word families to expand your vocabulary. Can you find the noun form of the vocabulary word *believe*? Use your dictionary.

1. My father's business is very <u>successful</u>. He has many customers.

2. When my soccer team won the <u>championship</u>, I was very excited.

3. She is a <u>poor</u> student because she never does her homework.

4. My aunt had a long <u>career</u> in education. She was a teacher for 35 years.

5. My dream is to <u>turn</u> my garage <u>into</u> an exercise room.

6. Mark is a very <u>strong</u> tennis player. He almost always wins.

7. I <u>believe</u> that good schools are important for children.

8. Carlos is very intelligent. He is the <u>top</u> math student in our school.

a. _____ (*adjective*) best

b. _____ (*adjective*) powerful; not weak

c. _____ (*noun*) a job you learn and do for many years

d. _____ (*adjective*) doing something well

e. _____ (*verb phrase*) to change and become different

f. _____ (*adjective*) bad; not very good

g. _____ (*verb*) to think that something is true

h. _____ (*noun*) a competition to find the best team in a sport

iQ ONLINE **B.** Go online for more practice with the vocabulary.

C. **PREVIEW** Before you read about a basketball coach, think about words related to the topic. Which words do you think are in the article? Underline the words.

baseball	court	field	lose	play
players	score	soccer	team	win

D. **QUICK WRITE** Write a few sentences about a coach or teacher you know. How does the person help players or students? Does the person have a good job? Why or why not? Use this section for your Unit Assignment.

WORK WITH THE READING

A. Read the article and find information about what events change our lives.

An Extraordinary Coach

1   About 30 years ago, a **successful** young basketball coach made a big decision. At that time, Tara VanDerveer was the coach for the best college basketball team in the U.S.—Ohio State University. The team won 110 games and four **championships** in five years. In 1985, Stanford University asked VanDerveer to be their basketball coach. Her friends and family thought she should stay at Ohio State. Stanford University was one of the best universities in the U.S., but it had a very **poor** basketball team. Her friends asked her, "Why do you want to leave your terrific job? At Ohio State, you have a wonderful **career**. Stanford will never become a great team." But VanDerveer knew she could make a great team, and she wanted to show others. "It was kind of like the ultimate[1] challenge," VanDerveer says.

2   In 1985, VanDerveer started coaching at Stanford University. Her goal was to **turn** the Stanford players **into** great athletes.

Tara VanDerveer

___
[1] **ultimate:** hardest, most difficult

At first, the players didn't have very **strong** basketball skills. But VanDerveer was an extraordinary coach, and she **believed** that her players could become winners. She was right. After five years, the team won a national championship. VanDerveer and her Stanford team continued to have many successful years.

3   In 1995, VanDerveer took a one-year break from Stanford. She coached the U.S. women's basketball team in the 1996 Summer Olympics. Her team won the gold medal. After that, VanDerveer wrote a book about her experience. She wrote about her life as a women's basketball coach and the fight to win the gold medal.

4   Today the Stanford team is one of the best teams in the country. In 2013, VanDerveer

players from the Stanford women's basketball team

celebrated the 900th win in her career as a coach. She is happy about her decision to move to Stanford. She enjoys coaching some of the most intelligent basketball players in the country and turning them into **top** athletes.

B. Read the sentences. Number them in the correct order from 1 to 6.

____ a.   She decided to accept the job at Stanford University.

____ b.   She coached the U.S. team in the Olympics.

____ c.   Stanford offered her a coaching job.

____ d.   Her friends and family thought moving was a bad idea.

____ e.   She coached her 900th winning game.

____ f.   She was a successful coach at Ohio State University.

C. Complete each statement with information from the article.

1. When VanDerveer was the basketball coach at _____,

    it was the top team in the United States.

2. Stanford University was famous for its academic program, but not for

    its _____.

3. VanDerveer said that she accepted the job at Stanford because it was the

    ultimate _____.

4. _____ years after VanDerveer became Stanford's coach, the team won a national championship.

5. In 1996, she coached the _____ team.

6. VanDerveer is happy with her decision to leave her job at _____.

D. Answer these questions. Write complete sentences.

1. When did Stanford offer VanDerveer the job?

   _____

2. Why did VanDerveer accept the job?

   _____

3. Why did her friends and family think she made a bad decision?

   _____

4. When did she take a break from college coaching?

   _____

5. What medal did her team win at the Olympics?

   _____

an Olympic gold medal

E. Read these phrases about Tara VanDerveer. For each phrase, write *D* (decision) or *E* (event). A decision is a choice. An event is something that happens.

1. _E_ 1996 Summer Olympics

2. ___ took a break in 1995

3. ___ accepted job at Stanford

4. ___ team won four championships

5. ___ team won the gold medal

6. ___ wrote a book

F. For VanDerveer, what was probably the most important event? What was the most important decision?

_____

_____

 G. Go online to read _Remembering Milestones_ and check your comprehension.

WRITE WHAT YOU THINK

A. Discuss these questions with a partner or in a group. Look back at your Quick Write on page 142. Think about what you learned.

1. VanDerveer is a very strong person. Give two examples from her life that show her personal strength.

2. A competitive person likes a good challenge. Do you think VanDerveer is a competitive person? Why?

iQ ONLINE **B.** Go online to watch the video about a soccer team. Then check your comprehension.

> **mines** (n.) very big holes in the ground, where people work to get special stones
>
> **refugees** (n.) people who must leave their country because of danger
>
> **soldiers** (n.) people in an army
>
> **war zones** (n.) areas where there is fighting between countries or groups

VIDEO VOCABULARY

Critical Thinking (Tip)

In Activity C, you **compare** Wood, VanDerveer, and Mufleh to people you know about. Connecting new information to information you already know helps you understand ideas better.

C. Think about the unit video, Reading 1, and Reading 2 as you discuss these questions. Then choose one question and write an answer.

1. Can you think of a person like John Wood, Tara VanDerveer, or Luma Mufleh? How is the person similar to Wood, VanDerveer, or Mufleh? What does/did this person do?

2. Are you more interested in John Wood, Tara VanDerveer, or Luma Mufleh? Why? Where can you find more information about this person?

Most words have several meanings. When you use a dictionary, first find the word and the correct word form (noun, verb, adjective, etc.). Then scan the definitions. **Choose the correct definition** for the context of the word. (The context is the sentence the word is in.)

☐ Wood wanted to give something valuable to children—education.

Read the definitions. The correct definition for the context in the sentence above is definition 2.

> **val·u·a·ble** 🔑 /ˈvælyəbl/ *adjective*
> **1** worth a lot of money: *Is this ring valuable?*
> **2** very useful: *The book contains some valuable information.*

All dictionary entries are from the *Oxford Basic American Dictionary for learners of English* © Oxford University Press 2011.

A. Read the sentences on page 147. Then scan the definitions below. Write the correct definition number next to each sentence.

> **con·tin·ue** 🔑 /kənˈtɪnyu/ *verb* (con·tin·ues, con·tin·u·ing, con·tin·ued)
> **1** to not stop happening or doing something: *If the pain continues, see your doctor.* • *The rain continued all afternoon.*
> **2** to start again after stopping: *Let's have lunch now and continue the meeting this afternoon.*
> **3** to go farther in the same direction: *We continued along the path until we came to the river.*

> **or·gan·i·za·tion** 🔑 /ˌɔrgənəˈzeɪʃn/ *noun*
> **1** [*count*] a group of people who work together for a special purpose: *He works for an organization that helps old people.*
> **2** [*noncount*] the activity of planning or arranging something; the way that something is planned or arranged: *She's busy with the organization of her daughter's wedding.*

> **dream¹** 🔑 /drim/ *noun* [*count*]
> **1** pictures or events that happen in your mind when you are asleep: *I had a dream about school last night.* ➷ Look at **nightmare**.
> **2** something nice that you hope for: *His dream was to give up his job and live in the country.*

> **poor** 🔑 /pʊr/ *adjective* (poor·er, poor·est)
> **1** with very little money: *She was too poor to buy clothes for her children.* • *She gave her life to helping the poor* (= poor people). ➷ The noun is **poverty**. ➷ ANTONYM **rich**
> **2** a word that you use when you feel sad because someone has problems: *Poor Tina! She's not feeling well.*
> **3** bad: *My grandfather is in very poor health.*

___ a. Wood's **dream** was to bring books and education to children around the world.

___ b. In 2000, he started an **organization**, Room to Read.

___ c. Stanford University had a very **poor** basketball team.

___ d. VanDerveer **continues** to coach, bringing top high school players to the university.

Tip for Success

Some words have the same word form for the noun and the verb. For example: *I had a dream about school last night. I often dream about school.*

B. Complete each sentence with one of the words from Activity A. Write the correct definition number next to each sentence.

_2_ a. The school sports day was terrific. The ____organization____ of the event was excellent.

___ b. My grandfather's family was very _____. They didn't have much money.

___ c. The boy woke up in the middle of the night. He had a bad _____.

___ d. After you turn on First Street, _____ straight ahead to the traffic light.

___ e. Sam is a _____ driver. He drives too fast, and he doesn't stop at red lights.

___ f. This _____ helps residents improve their neighborhood.

neighborhood improvements

___ g. Let's take a break for lunch. We can _____ studying for the test after lunch.

___ h. My _____ did not seem possible, but I finally won a school race.

iQ ONLINE **C. Go online for more practice using the dictionary.**

WRITING

UNIT OBJECTIVE

At the end of this unit, you are going to write about an important event in your life. Your sentences will include information from the readings, the unit video, and your own ideas.

Grammar | Simple past with regular and irregular verbs

The simple past describes completed actions in the past.

> Last summer, he **decided** to attend a community college.
> I **graduated** from high school last year.

Many verbs have irregular past forms. (They don't end in -*ed*.) For a list, see page 162.

Irregular past forms

come	**came**	give	**gave**	leave	**left**	spend	**spent**
do	**did**	go	**went**	make	**made**	take	**took**
get	**got**	have	**had**	see	**saw**	write	**wrote**

Affirmative statements

subject	verb	
I / You / We / They	**moved**	to this city in 2009.
He / She / It	**came**	to my house last night.

- For affirmative statements, use the same past form for all subjects.

Negative statements

subject	*did + not*	verb	
I / You / We / They	**did not**	**continue**	the game.
He / She / It	**didn't**	**come**	to class yesterday.

- For negative statements, use *did not* or *didn't* + the base verb for both regular and irregular verbs.

Yes/No questions				Short answers	
did	subject	verb		*yes*	*no*
Did	they	**move**	to Miami?	Yes, they **did**.	No, they **didn't**.
Did	she	**come**	here?	Yes, she **did**.	No, she **didn't**.

Information questions				Answers
wh- word	*did*	subject	verb	past verb
Who		you	**see?**	I **saw** the coach.
What	**did**	the coach	**say?**	She **said**, "No."
Where		the players	**go?**	They **went** to the gym.

A. Complete the sentences. Use the correct form of the irregular verb. Some sentences need the negative form.

1. I _____*didn't meet*_____ (not, meet) my friends today. I met them last night.

2. Last night Mika _____ (give) her friend some advice about college.

3. Mika _____ (tell) her friend about her college classes.

4. Sarah's family _____ (come) to this country five years ago.

5. My team _____ (win) the championship last year. We were very excited.

6. We _____ (not, leave) at 10:30. We left at noon.

7. Last year, Emma _____ (have) trouble with her math class.

8. David _____ (not, speak) English when he came here. He spoke Spanish.

9. I _____ (send) you an email last night.

10. Yesterday Sam _____ (take) a driving test. Fortunately, he passed it.

a driving test

B. Complete the questions with *you* and the correct form of the verb. Then answer the questions. Use complete sentences.

1. Where _____*did you go*_____ (go) yesterday?

   ___*I went to school, and in the afternoon I went to soccer practice.*___

2. _____ (take) a test last week?

   _____

3. Who _____ (speak) with last night?

_____

4. _____ (have) lunch at school yesterday?

_____

5. Who _____ (send) an email to yesterday?

_____

6. How _____ (get) to school today?

_____

7. How much money _____ (spend) yesterday?

_____

8. Who _____ (see) last weekend?

_____

C. **Check each sentence for the correct simple past verb. If it is not correct, fix the errors. Write C next to the sentences that are correct.**

_____ 1. I have a very funny dream last night.

_____ 2. My father graduate from a top university.

_____ 3. He no spend very much money during his trip last month.

_____ 4. I got a package in the mail yesterday.

_____ 5. It take a long time to get home last night.

_____ 6. We gave books to the school library.

_____ 7. She no did do her homework last night.

_____ 8. My grandmother make a special cake for my birthday last week.

_____ 9. They didn't go to the championship game.

_____ 10. I am seeing my friends in the park yesterday.

 **D.** **Go online for more practice using the simple past with regular and irregular verbs.**

E. **Go online for the grammar expansion.**

A simple sentence has one main idea. A simple sentence can have two subjects. It can also have two verbs, using *and*.

subject + subject verb

My friends **and** I play soccer on the weekend.

subject verb + verb

Alan studies in the afternoon **and** works at night.

Each simple sentence has one main idea, even though there are two subjects and two verbs.

In a **compound sentence**, <u>both</u> parts of the sentence have a subject and a verb. There is a comma before *and*.

subject verb   subject verb

Susan is a top student, **and** she is an excellent tennis player.

subject verb   subject + subject verb

I went to the coffee shop, **and** my friend and I talked for a long time.

A. Read each simple sentence. Label each subject (*S*) and verb (*V*). Underline *and*. Then write the number of subjects and verbs.

1. My brother <u>and</u> I went to the same university.

    Subjects: _2_ Verbs: _1_

2. Jose made a good decision and got a degree in accounting.

    Subjects: ____ Verbs: ____

3. He started his career in banking three years ago.

    Subjects: ____ Verbs: ____

4. He worked long hours and took some special classes.

    Subjects: ____ Verbs: ____

5. In one class, he and his classmates learned leadership skills.

    Subjects: ____ Verbs: ____

6. Last year, Jose became an assistant manager at his bank.

    Subjects: ____ Verbs: ____

B. Read the sentences. Underline *and*. Label each sentence a simple sentence (*SS*) or a compound sentence (*CS*).

____ 1. Tara VanDerveer was born in 1953 in Boston, Massachusetts.

____ 2. She attended Indiana State University.

____ 3. Tara majored in sociology, and she was a top basketball player.

____ 4. After college, she had several jobs and moved several times.

____ 5. In 1985, she accepted a position at Stanford University, and she moved to California.

____ 6. Her decision changed her life, and she created a great team.

____ 7. Today she feels very good about her decision, and her players are thankful to have such an excellent coach.

C. Read these sentences from Reading 1. Add commas to the compound sentences.

1. But that year, John Wood made a promise and it changed his life completely.

2. Wood had no salary and the organization's office was in his home.

3. He had to raise a lot of money and hire good people.

4. Wood had excellent business skills and Room to Read became a very strong organization.

5. Many people became excited about Wood's dream and Room to Read grew quickly.

6. In the first ten years, Room to Read helped five million children and built more than 11,000 libraries.

D. Combine each pair of simple sentences into a compound sentence. Include a comma before *and*.

1. He met Jane in college. They got married after graduation.

   He met Jane in college, and they got married after graduation.

2. Richard joined the organization in 2010. He became a vice president five years later.

   _____

3. Last year, I studied very hard. I became a top science student by the end of the year.

_____

4. The brothers have a successful restaurant business. Many family members work for them.

_____

5. I promised my family a delicious dinner. They loved everything that I made.

_____

6. The scholarship was a great opportunity. I accepted it right away.

_____

7. My mother continued to study at night. She received her diploma last year.

_____

E. **Write compound sentences. Use the words and your own ideas.**

1. my brother gave me / I

   My brother gave me a new dictionary, and I use it every day.

2. my friend gave me / I

   _____

3. my parents met / they

   _____

4. I read about / I decided to

   _____

5. I got a letter in the mail / I was

   _____

6. I am a strong / I can

   _____

 F. **Go online for more practice with sentences with *and*.**

In this assignment, you are going to write about an important event in your life. Think about the Unit Question, "What events change our lives?" Use the readings, the unit video, and your work in this unit. Look at the Self-Assessment checklist below.

iQ ONLINE Go to the Online Writing Tutor for a writing model and alternate Unit Assignments.

A. BRAINSTORM Follow these steps.

1. Make a timeline of some events in your life.

was born in Riyadh   moved to Istanbul, Turkey   family bought a house

| 1992 | 1998 | 2001 | 2004 | 2007 |

2. Circle two important events in your timeline.

3. Explain your timeline to a partner. Discuss the two important events.

iQ ONLINE **B. WRITE** Choose one event from your **BRAINSTORM** in Activity A. Answer these questions with complete sentences. Go to *iQ Online* to use the Online Writing Tutor.

1. When did it happen?   4. What happened?

2. Where did it happen?   5. How did you feel?

3. Who was there?   6. Why was it an important event?

iQ ONLINE **C. REVISE** Review your sentences with a partner. Read your partner's sentences. Then go online and use the Peer Review worksheet. Discuss the review with your partner.

D. EDIT AND REWRITE Complete the Self-Assessment checklist. Make final changes to your sentences. Be prepared to hand in your work or discuss it in class.

SELF-ASSESSMENT		
Yes	No	
☐	☐	Do you use compound sentences with *and*?
☐	☐	Are your verbs in the simple past correct?
☐	☐	Do you include vocabulary from the unit?
☐	☐	Does every sentence have correct punctuation?

1. What is something new you learned in this unit?

2. Look back at the Unit Question—What events change our lives? Is your answer different now than when you started the unit? If yes, how is it different?

TRACK YOUR SUCCESS

Circle the words and phrases you have learned in this unit.

Nouns	**Verbs**	**Adjectives**
career 🔑	believe 🔑	poor 🔑
championship	continue 🔑	strong 🔑
dream 🔑	decide 🔑	successful 🔑
opportunity 🔑	promise 🔑	top 🔑
organization 🔑	**Verb phrase**	valuable 🔑
	turn (something) into (something)	**Adverb**
		even 🔑

🔑 Oxford 2000 keywords

AWL Academic Word List

Check (✓) the skills you learned. If you need more work on a skill, refer to the page(s) in parentheses.

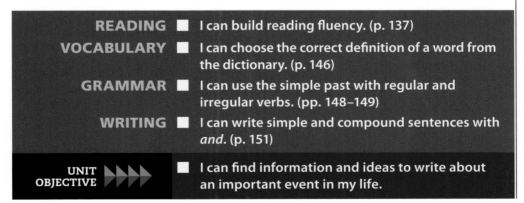

READING	☐ I can build reading fluency. (p. 137)
VOCABULARY	☐ I can choose the correct definition of a word from the dictionary. (p. 146)
GRAMMAR	☐ I can use the simple past with regular and irregular verbs. (pp. 148–149)
WRITING	☐ I can write simple and compound sentences with *and*. (p. 151)
UNIT OBJECTIVE ▶▶▶▶	☐ I can find information and ideas to write about an important event in my life.

AUDIO TRACK LIST

Q: Skills for Success Second Edition audio can be found in the Media Center.

Follow these steps:

Step 1: Go to iQOnlinePractice.com.

Step 2: Click on the Media Center icon.

Step 3: Choose to stream or download the audio file you select. Not all audio files are available for download.

Class Audio

Unit	Page	Listen	Download
Unit 1			
1	3	The Q Classroom	⬇
1	6	Work With the Reading	⬇
1	13	Work With the Reading	⬇
Unit 2			
2	28	The Q Classroom	⬇
2	32	Work With the Reading	⬇
2	38	Work With the Reading	⬇
Unit 3			
3	55	The Q Classroom	⬇
3	58	Work With the Reading	⬇
3	65	Work With the Reading	

Back

Unit	Activity	Track File Name
Unit 1	The Q Classroom, p. 2	Q2e_00_RW_U01_ Q_Classroom.mp3
	Work With the Reading, p. 6	Q2e_00_RW_U01_ Reading1.mp3
Unit 2	The Q Classroom, p. 21	Q2e_00_RW_U02_Q_Classroom.mp3
	Work With the Reading, p. 23	Q2e_00_RW_U02_Reading1.mp3
Unit 3	The Q Classroom, p. 37	Q2e_00_RW_U03_Q_Classroom.mp3
	Work With the Reading, p. 39	Q2e_00_RW_U03_Reading1.mp3
Unit 4	The Q Classroom, p. 53	Q2e_00_RW_U04_Q_Classroom.mp3
	Work With the Reading, p. 56	Q2e_00_RW_U04_Reading1.mp3
Unit 5	The Q Classroom, p. 68	Q2e_00_RW_U05_Q_Classroom.mp3
	Work With the Reading, p. 72	Q2e_00_RW_U05_Reading1.mp3
	Work With the Reading, p. 77	Q2e_00_RW_U05_Reading2.mp3
Unit 6	The Q Classroom, p. 90	Q2e_00_RW_U06_Q_Classroom.mp3
	Work With the Reading, p. 93	Q2e_00_RW_U06_Reading1.mp3
	Work With the Reading, p. 99	Q2e_00_RW_U06_Reading2.mp3
Unit 7	The Q Classroom, p. 113	Q2e_00_RW_U07_Q_Classroom.mp3
	Work With the Reading, p. 115	Q2e_00_RW_U07_Reading1.mp3
	Work With the Reading, p. 122	Q2e_00_RW_U07_Reading2.mp3
Unit 8	The Q Classroom, p. 134	Q2e_00_RW_U08_Q_Classroom.mp3
	Work With the Reading, p. 138	Q2e_00_RW_U08_Reading1.mp3
	Work With the Reading, p. 142	Q2e_00_RW_U08_Reading2.mp3

Authors

Jennifer Bixby holds an M.A. in TESOL from Boston University. She is a senior development editor for EF Englishtown, editing and writing online ELT content. Jennifer has taught students of various ages in Colombia, Japan, and the U.S in a wide variety of programs, including community colleges and intensive English programs. She has presented at numerous conferences on the topics of materials development and the teaching of reading and writing. She is coauthor with Nigel Caplan of *Inside Writing* 2 and 4 published by Oxford University Press.

Joe McVeigh holds a B.A. in English and American Literature from Brown University and an M.A. in TESOL from Biola University. He has taught at Middlebury College, the University of Southern California, the California Institute of Technology, and California State University, Los Angeles. Joe has also lived and worked overseas in the U.K., Hungary, China, India, Chile, and the Middle East. He has presented nationally and internationally on topics including methods and techniques for teaching English, intercultural communication, and curriculum development. He works independently as a consultant, teacher trainer, workshop presenter, and author.

Series Consultants

ONLINE INTEGRATION

Chantal Hemmi holds an Ed.D. TEFL and is a Japan-based teacher trainer and curriculum designer. Since leaving her position as Academic Director of the British Council in Tokyo, she has been teaching at the Center for Language Education and Research at Sophia University on an EAP/CLIL program offered for undergraduates. She delivers lectures and teacher trainings throughout Japan, Indonesia, and Malaysia.

COMMUNICATIVE GRAMMAR

Nancy Schoenfeld holds an M.A. in TESOL from Biola University in La Mirada, California, and has been an English language instructor since 2000. She has taught ESL in California and Hawaii, and EFL in Thailand and Kuwait. She has also trained teachers in the United States and Indonesia. Her interests include teaching vocabulary, extensive reading, and student motivation. She is currently an English Language Instructor at Kuwait University.

WRITING

Marguerite Ann Snow holds a Ph.D. in Applied Linguistics from UCLA. She teaches in the TESOL M.A. program in the Charter College of Education at California State University, Los Angeles. She was a Fulbright scholar in Hong Kong and Cyprus. In 2006, she received the President's Distinguished Professor award at Cal State, LA. She has trained EFL teachers in Algeria, Argentina, Brazil, Egypt, Libya, Morocco, Pakistan, Peru, Spain, and Turkey. She is the author/editor of publications in the areas of integrated content, English for academic purposes, and standards for English teaching and learning. She recently served as a co-editor of *Teaching English as a Second or Foreign Language* (4th ed.).

VOCABULARY

Cheryl Boyd Zimmerman is a Professor at California State University, Fullerton. She specializes in second-language vocabulary acquisition, an area in which she is widely published. She teaches graduate courses on second-language acquisition, culture, vocabulary, and the fundamentals of TESOL and is a frequent invited speaker on topics related to vocabulary teaching and learning. She is the author of *Word Knowledge: A Vocabulary Teacher's Handbook* and Series Director of *Inside Reading, Inside Writing,* and *Inside Listening and Speaking,* all published by Oxford University Press.

ASSESSMENT

Lawrence J. Zwier holds an M.A. in TESL from the University of Minnesota. He is currently the Associate Director for Curriculum Development at the English Language Center at Michigan State University in East Lansing. He has taught ESL/EFL in the United States, Saudi Arabia, Malaysia, Japan, and Singapore.

iQ ONLINE extends your learning beyond the classroom. This online content is specifically designed for you! *iQ Online* gives you flexible access to essential content.

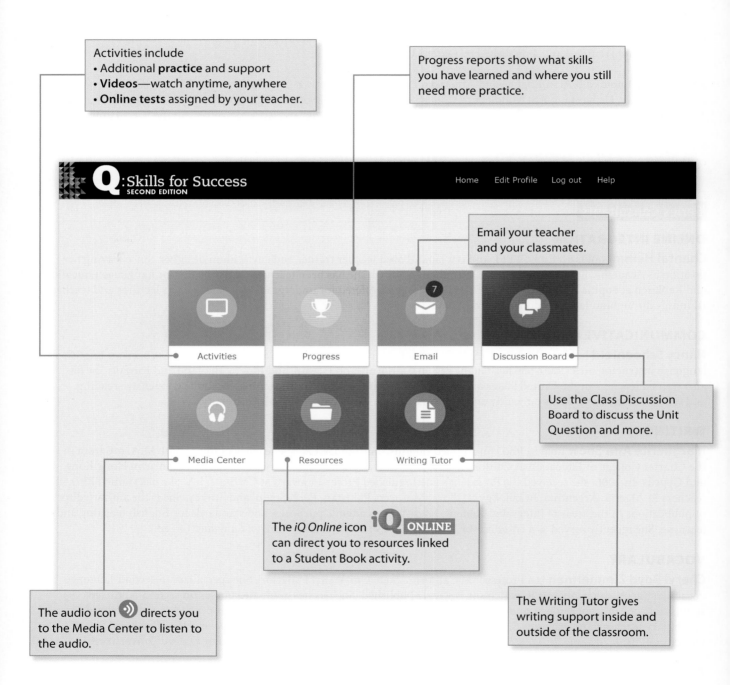

Activities include
• Additional **practice** and support
• **Videos**—watch anytime, anywhere
• **Online tests** assigned by your teacher.

Progress reports show what skills you have learned and where you still need more practice.

Email your teacher and your classmates.

Use the Class Discussion Board to discuss the Unit Question and more.

The *iQ Online* icon **iQ ONLINE** can direct you to resources linked to a Student Book activity.

The audio icon directs you to the Media Center to listen to the audio.

The Writing Tutor gives writing support inside and outside of the classroom.

Q:Skills for Success
SECOND EDITION
Home   Edit Profile   Log out   Help

Activities   Progress   Email   Discussion Board

Media Center   Resources   Writing Tutor

SEE THE INSIDE FRONT COVER FOR HOW TO REGISTER FOR *iQ ONLINE* FOR THE FIRST TIME.

Take Control of Your Learning

You have the choice of where and how you complete the activities. Access your activities and view your progress at any time.

Your teacher may

- assign *iQ Online* as homework,
- do the activities with you in class, or
- let you complete the activities at a pace that is right for you.

iQ Online makes it easy to access everything you need.

Set Clear Goals

STEP 1 If it is your first time, look through the site. See what learning opportunities are available.

STEP 2 The Student Book provides the framework and purpose for each online activity. Before going online, notice the goal of the exercises you are going to do.

STEP 3 Stay on top of your work, following the teacher's instructions.

STEP 4 Use *iQ Online* for review. You can use the materials any time. It is easy for you to do follow-up activities when you have missed a class or want to review.

Manage Your Progress

The activities in *iQ Online* are designed for you to work independently. You can become a confident learner by monitoring your progress and reviewing the activities at your own pace. You may already be used to working online, but if you are not, go to your teacher for guidance.

Check 'View Reports' to monitor your progress. The reports let you track your own progress at a glance. Think about your own performance and set new goals that are right for you, following the teacher's instructions.

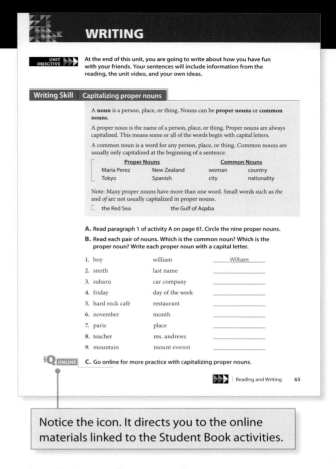

Notice the icon. It directs you to the online materials linked to the Student Book activities.

iQ Online is a research-based solution specifically designed for English language learners that extends learning beyond the classroom. I hope these steps help you make the most of this essential content.

C. N. Hemm

Chantal Hemmi, EdD TEFL
Center for Language Education and Research
Sophia University, Japan

VOCABULARY LIST AND CEFR CORRELATION

🔑 The keywords of the **Oxford 2000** have been carefully selected by a group of language experts and experienced teachers as the words which should receive priority in vocabulary study because of their importance and usefulness.

AWL The Academic Word List is the most principled and widely accepted list of academic words. Averil Coxhead gathered information from academic materials across the academic disciplines to create this word list.

The Common European Framework of Reference for Languages (CEFR) provides a basic description of what language learners have to do to use language effectively. The system contains six reference levels: **A1, A2, B1, B2, C1, C2.** CEFR leveling provided by the Word Family Framework, created by Richard West and published by the British Council. http://www.learnenglish.org.uk/wff/

UNIT 1

average *(adj.)* 🔑, A2
describe *(v.)* 🔑, A1
fashionable *(adj.)* 🔑, A1
messy *(adj.)* 🔑, A2
personality *(n.)* 🔑, B1
serious *(adj.)* 🔑, A1

UNIT 2

academic *(adj.)* 🔑 AWL, A1
break *(n.)* 🔑, A2
last *(v.)* 🔑, A2
uniform *(n.)* 🔑 AWL, A2
vacation *(n.)* 🔑, A1

UNIT 3

celebrate *(v.)* 🔑, A2
culture *(n.)* 🔑 AWL, A1
fresh *(adj.)* 🔑, A1
popular *(adj.)* 🔑, A1
prepare *(v.)* 🔑, A1
special *(adj.)* 🔑, A1
traditional *(adj.)* AWL, A1

UNIT 4

event *(n.)* 🔑, A1
expensive *(adj.)* 🔑, A1
guess *(v.)* 🔑, A1
invite *(v.)* 🔑, A2
nature *(n.)* 🔑, A1
program *(n.)* 🔑, A1
support *(v.)* 🔑, B1

UNIT 5

bright *(adj.)* 🔑, A1
calm *(adj.)* 🔑, A2
collect *(v.)* 🔑, A1
comfortable *(adj.)* 🔑, A2
design *(v.)* 🔑 AWL, A1
extra *(adj.)* 🔑, A1
however *(adv.)* 🔑, A1
modern *(adj.)* 🔑, A1
own *(v.)* 🔑, A1
share *(v.)* 🔑, A2
smell *(v.)* 🔑, B1
space *(n.)* 🔑, A1
view *(n.)* 🔑, A2

UNIT 6

become *(v.)* 🔑, A1
behavior *(n.)* 🔑, A1
break *(v.)* 🔑, A1
create *(v.)* 🔑 AWL, A1
expert *(n.)* 🔑 AWL, A2
give up *(phr. v.)* 🔑, B1
goal *(n.)* 🔑 AWL, A1
instead of *(phr.)* 🔑, A1
stress *(n.)* 🔑 AWL, A2
unfortunately *(adv.)* 🔑, A2

UNIT 7

characteristic *(n.)* 🔑, A2
complaint *(n.)* 🔑, A2
crime *(n.),* 🔑, A2
economy *(n.)* 🔑 AWL, A1
immigrant *(n.)* AWL, B1
impression *(n.)* 🔑, A2
improve *(v.)* 🔑, A1
international *(adj.)* 🔑 AWL, A1
market *(n.)* 🔑, A1
opinion *(n.)* 🔑, A1